the sacred art of
LOVINGKINDNESS
preparing to practice

Rabbi Rami Shapiro

Foreword by Marcia Ford

Walking Together, Finding the Way
SKYLIGHT PATHS® Publishing
Woodstock, Vermont

The Sacred Art of Lovingkindness:
Preparing to Practice

2008 Third Printing
2007 Second Printing
2006 First Printing
© 2006 by Rami Shapiro

For information regarding permission to reprint material from this book, please write or fax your request to SkyLight Paths Publishing, Permissions Department, at the address / fax number listed below, or e-mail your request to permissions@skylightpaths.com.

Library of Congress Cataloging-in-Publication Data
Shapiro, Rami M.
The sacred art of lovingkindness : preparing to practice / Rami Shapiro ; foreword by Marcia Ford.
p. cm. — (Preparing to practice)
Includes bibliographical references and index.
ISBN-13: 978-1-59473-151-8 (pbk.)
ISBN-10: 1-59473-151-9 (pbk.)
1. Kindness. 2. Kindness—Religious aspects. 3. Compassion. 4. Compassion—Religious aspects. 5. Conduct of life. 6. Spiritual life. I. Title. II. Series.
BJ1533.K5S53 2006
177'.7—dc22
2006008338

10 9 8 7 6 5 4 3

SkyLight Paths Publishing is creating a place where people of different spiritual traditions come together for challenge and inspiration, a place where we can help each other understand the mystery that lies at the heart of our existence.

SkyLight Paths sees both believers and seekers as a community that increasingly transcends traditional boundaries of religion and denomination—people wanting to learn from each other, *walking together, finding the way.*

Manufactured in the United States of America
Cover Design: Tim Holtz
SkyLight Paths, "Walking Together, Finding the Way," and colophon are trademarks of LongHill Partners, Inc., registered in the U.S. Patent and Trademark Office.

Walking Together, Finding the Way®
Published by SkyLight Paths Publishing
A Division of LongHill Partners, Inc.
Sunset Farm Offices, Route 4, P.O. Box 237
Woodstock, VT 05091
Tel: (802) 457-4000   Fax: (802) 457-4004
www.skylightpaths.com

This book is dedicated to
all those friends and teachers—some mentioned in these pages,
many more not—who through their lives
have shown me what lovingkindness truly is.

CONTENTS

FOREWORD

Lovingkindness is one of those topics I love to read about. It's such a *lofty* quality. I'll finish reading a book about it, and I'll sigh, wishing I could be like some celebrated Buddhist leader whose very name is synonymous with lovingkindness. Who wouldn't want that? The problem is, I haven't put much of what I've read into practice. Oh, I've exercised my version of lovingkindness for a day or two at a stretch but, soon enough, I revert to my baser nature and wish that all manner of evil would befall the unbelievably rude guy who cut in front of me at the post office.

I recently realized that I clearly needed to take action if I was ever going to integrate this noble quality into my very ordinary life. So I did what I usually do when action is required: I read yet another book. But this time was different. This time the book's author gave me two essential tools for learning to practice lovingkindness—a series of practical exercises that I would actually want to do, and the hope that cultivating a life characterized by lovingkindness is not beyond the reach of a mere mortal such as me. For both, I owe a considerable debt to Rabbi Rami Shapiro. *The Sacred Art of Lovingkindness* has accomplished what no other book has: it has encouraged me and convinced me that the person I want to be is a person I can indeed become.

I suspect, too, that it's Rabbi Rami's own humanness that sets his book apart from so many others on the topic. He admits that he has not mastered this sacred art; he claims to be more like a "kindergartner with finger paints." Finger painting can get pretty messy, as I recall, but it seems there was always one kid in the class who was just as messy as the rest of us but managed to create a really cool painting with all kinds of swirls and curlicues and squiggly lines. My guess is that in kindergarten, the future Rabbi Rami was that one kid—because here, he creates a beautiful picture of lovingkindness as it can be lived out successfully in the everyday, messy lives of harried, distracted, stressed-out Americans.

In truth, he paints thirteen pictures, each representing one of Judaism's Thirteen Attributes of Lovingkindness, a teaching I had never encountered in thirty-plus years of studying religion and covering it as a journalist. He adds richness and depth to those pictures by drawing from all the major faith traditions and incorporating their teachings and practices into his own understanding of lovingkindness. And he does so with such a generosity of spirit that I have to wonder how he can possibly paint—or write—with his arms spread out in a welcoming, open gesture.

It's openness, of course, that enables us to practice lovingkindness—openness to God, first and foremost. When we choose to lean into God, to immerse our lives in the kingdom of a God of love and compassion and kindness and truth and forgiveness and grace and so much more, we make ourselves vulnerable to acquiring those very same qualities. Every moment of every day we have the God-given capacity to choose love over hate, compassion over apathy, kindness over cruelty. In those moments, we see all too clearly whether our openness to God has made us open to change. Because if we think we can practice lovingkindness without allowing God to transform us, we are truly deceived. Lovingkindness doesn't exactly come naturally to most of us.

Open to God, open to change, and finally, open to others. This is where things get thorny. We could live quite nicely in that lofty realm of lovingkindness if it wasn't for all these blasted people in our lives. But that's where lovingkindness is lived out, in our relationships with others. All of our relationships—the good, the bad, the indifferent. If we're honest with ourselves, most of us would have to admit that we're not all that great at treating the people we *love* with lovingkindness; how on earth can we be expected to treat people we *dislike* better than the way we're now treating our loved ones? We can't—at least, not until we live in that place where heaven and earth meet, where our lives are so entwined with God that God's lovingkindness becomes ours. Thankfully, finding that place just became easier, because in the following pages the good rabbi shows us how to assimilate into our lives the very spiritual practices that will lead us there. Even better, he shows us how he applies these practices in his own busy, twenty-first century, down-to-earth life, leaving us without excuse. And he does so with humility and humor, two qualities that for me rank right up there with lovingkindness.

The nature of my work has me reading well over a hundred books a year. I have precious little time and even less inclination to read any book more than once. But I've now read *The Sacred Art of Lovingkindness* twice—even *before* its publication—and I fully intend to read it a third time this year, once I badger my reading group into ignoring our next selected book and replacing it with this one. By then I'm confident I will have mastered the sacred art of badgering others graciously.

I encourage you to make time for at least one reading. Without question, that one reading will provide you with a wealth of new ideas to consider, reflections to meditate on, spiritual activities to practice. There's enough here to last a lifetime—a lifetime brimming with lovingkindness.

Shalom.

—Marcia Ford

INTRODUCTION:
WHAT IS
LOVINGKINDNESS?

*It's a bit embarrassing to have been concerned with
the human problem all one's life and find at the end
that one has no more to offer [by way of advice] than
this: Try to be a little kinder.*

—*Aldous Huxley*

How can I write a book about something I myself have not mastered? When it comes to the sacred art of lovingkindness I am neither a Rembrandt nor a Picasso. I am more like a kindergartner with finger paints. My rationale for writing this book is simply that I believe there may be some merit in exploring this art from the standpoint of an amateur. There will be no preaching, no moral one-upmanship, no hierarchy of master and student. Instead, I will share my own many-detoured journey on this path, offer a few signposts as teachings along the way, and highlight practices from a variety of religious traditions that aid me in my struggle to make the world a bit more kind for my having been born into it.

The question at the heart of this book is this: Will you engage this moment with kindness or with cruelty, with love or with fear, with generosity or scarcity, with a joyous heart or an embittered one?

This is your choice and no one can make it for you. If you choose kindness, love, generosity, and joy, then you will discover in that choice the Kingdom of God, heaven, nirvana, this-worldly salvation. If you choose cruelty, fear, scarcity, and bitterness, then you will discover in that choice the hellish states of which so many religions speak. These are not ontological realities tucked away somewhere in space—these are existential realities playing out in your own mind. Heaven and hell are both inside of you. It is your choice that determines just where you will reside.

In writing this book I made the choice for heaven, and having done so, I went in search of tools for living it. As a rabbi it was only natural for me to look first to Judaism in search of these tools, and what I found there provides the skeleton for what you will read here. Judaism speaks of Thirteen Attributes, or aspects, of Lovingkindness, and each of these is explored in the chapters that follow. Some chapters are devoted to one attribute alone; others address more.

The attributes come from the book of Exodus. Moses asks to see God's glory, how godliness is manifest in the world (Exodus 33:18). God agrees, saying, "I will make all My goodness pass before you" (Exodus 33:19). God passes before Moses and calls out each aspect of goodness in turn: (1) realizing the divinity of self, (2) realizing the divinity of other, (3) cultivating creativity, (4) engendering compassion, (5) finding grace, (6) acting with equanimity, (7) creating kindness, (8) bringing forth truth, (9) preserving kindness, (10) forgiving iniquity, (11) forgiving willfulness, (12) forgiving error, and (13) cleansing yourself of delusion. Together these are called the Thirteen Attributes of Lovingkindness. For the purposes of this book I have translated the attributes into practices in which you can engage and through which you can actualize God's glory through personal deeds of lovingkindness.

These attributes of lovingkindness are chanted during various worship services, especially during the High Holy Days of Rosh HaShanah (the Jewish New Year) and Yom Kippur (the Day of Atonement). This is to remind worshipers of God's infinite compassion and their obligation to manifest it in their own lives.

Outside of communal prayer, the Thirteen Attributes are used as a mantra for private meditation. In my daily meditation practice, I chant these attributes in Hebrew over and over, inviting them to take root in my psyche and transform me in their service. In addition to chanting all thirteen, I often focus on one attribute each week, giving special attention to the practices associated with it, so that I might continually strengthen my capacity to live this aspect of lovingkindness. At the end of a thirteen-week cycle, I begin all over again.

While not asking you to learn to chant the Thirteen Attributes of Lovingkindness, my goal in writing this book is to help you cultivate these attributes in your own life. In a sense, then, this book is a cookbook for lovingkindness, and it must supply you with recipes for making your life more loving and kind if it is to be of any real value to you. I have culled these recipes from a number of religious traditions. No one religion has a monopoly on lovingkindness, and each has something to offer those who have made the choice for heaven. I encourage you to study broadly in the world's religions and adapt what you need from wherever it is found.

It is not enough to be versed in only one religion. You are heir to the entire spectrum of human spirituality. While one of them may resonate more strongly within you than another, you can learn from them all and adapt practices from each to enrich your own capacity for lovingkindness. May this short book be for you a first step on the never-ending path of wisdom.

CHAPTER ONE

THE IMAGE AND LIKENESS OF GOD

Realizing the Divinity of Self, Realizing the Divinity of Others

The Tao that can be named is not the eternal Tao.
—*Tao Te Ching*

Days after the December 2004 tsunami took the lives of hundreds of thousands of people in Indonesia and elsewhere, the Gospel Music Association of America (GMA) teamed up with country, jazz, and hip-hop performers in Nashville to sponsor a tsunami relief concert. Since this was sponsored by the GMA, it made sense to the promoters to invite several local ministers to address the thousands of attendees. And, since this is the United States, they thought it wise to add a rabbi to the mix as well. I was lucky enough to get that invitation.

The concert began about forty-five minutes late. I spent this downtime sitting in a corner watching dozens of performers, almost all of whom were household names in the gospel and country music worlds, mingle with one another and mug for the cameras. I didn't know where the other clergypeople were, and no one seemed much interested in me, so I had lots of time to agonize over what I was going to say. I came up blank.

I wandered upstairs into the concert itself. The music was phenomenal, yet great care was taken to make sure no one forgot why we were there. When the first minister was called to the podium, he began his brief talk by saying that he had just returned from Indonesia, where his church was actively involved in relief efforts. He spoke not only from the heart but also from firsthand knowledge. I was moved and impressed.

About an hour and a half into the concert, the floor manager found me and gave me a ten-minute warning. A very serious young woman led me to the back of the stage, and I began to study the path I needed to walk in order to get to the podium. The floor was strewn with thick black cables and equipment cases, and I feared I would trip over something and end up delivering my speech facedown in a snake pit of rubber wire.

Suddenly the cohost for the evening, *Nashville Star*'s Kathy Mattea, called my name and my "handler" gently pushed me forward. I watched myself on the Jumbotron as I navigated my way to the podium.

For a moment I forgot that I hadn't yet settled on what to say. I was struck dumb. I had not been to Indonesia; I had not done anything to help anybody hurt by the tsunami; and I had never spoken to a crowd this large. The moment passed and I started to speak.

"There is one thing rabbis are trained to do, and that is to teach Torah. So let's study the Bible together for a few minutes. The book of Genesis tells us that we are created in the image and likeness of God. Yet when God actually creates us, Torah refers to us only as the image of God and not the likeness. Let's take a look at what these terms mean, and why the difference in the wording matters.

"What does it mean to be the image of God? Being the image of God means that we are God manifest. Just as a wave is the ocean extended in time and space, so each one of us is God extended in time and space.

"What does it mean to be the likeness of God? Being the likeness of God means that we have the potential to act in a godly manner. It means that we can, regardless of our ideology, theology, and politics, engage each moment and each other with lovingkindness.

"According to Genesis, God intends for us to be godly, to honor the image by living out the likeness. This is not a metaphor. The Hebrew Name of God, the four-letter Name Y-H-V-H, *yod-hey-vav-hey,* when written vertically takes on the shape of a human being. Each one of us is the Name of God incarnate."

At that point I asked everyone who could stand to stand. I asked them to turn and face a neighbor. Then, using the Jumbotron as my visual aide, I had them draw the Hebrew Name of God on each other's body.

"The letter *yod* is like a seven. Starting on the right side of your neighbor's forehead, run your finger across the forehead, then down the nose, over the lips to the chin. That is the letter *yod,* the first letter of God's Holy Name. Draw it, feel it on the body.

"The second letter of God's Name is *hey.* This letter is the shape of the shoulders and arms. Start with both hands on your partner's sternum and then draw a line outward across the shoulders and down both arms, leaving a slight space between the shoulder and elbow of the right arm.

"The third letter is *vav.* It runs down your torso or spinal column. Use your finger to draw a line from just below the sternum to the pelvis. Don't linger at the pelvis." Everyone laughed.

"The fourth and final letter of God's Name is another *hey.* Draw a line across your neighbor's hips and down both legs to the feet."

When everyone had a chance to draw and be drawn on, I said, "Now step back from your neighbor and visualize the

Name of God as their body. Don't imagine it is written on the body, or that it is glowing through from inside the body. The body itself is the Name of God. Now close your eyes and sense the same thing regarding your body. You are the Name of God. You are the image of God. Now open your eyes and tap as many people as you can reach on the forehead saying, 'Image of God!'"

The house lights came up and I watched in wonder as thousands of people joyfully shouted, "Image of God! Image of God!"

"Image of God," I said when most were seated, "but not yet the likeness of God. You are born the image of God, but living out the likeness of God is a choice. And you are making that choice right now. Here you are, thousands of you in this room, thousands more listening in by radio, to help people most of you have never met. The people struck by this tragedy don't look like you. They don't believe as you do. They don't share your culture, or speak your language, or listen to your music. They couldn't be more different. And yet here you are, your hearts broken over their tragedy, and your wallets and purses open to be of service in their recovery. Why? Because at moments such as these we do not see the other as stranger, but as neighbor; as the Image of God. And when we see the Image of God in others we cannot help but act out the likeness of God ourselves.

"We are here because the fact of human suffering is deeper and more compelling than any theology. We are here because when we root our reality in the body rather than the mind, in the facts of existence rather than the fantasies we spin about it, we know beyond any doubt that we are all the image of God. And this knowing compels us to act out the lovingkindness that is the heart of the likeness of God. Turn to your neighbors once more, tap them gently on the heart and whisper close to their ear, 'Likeness of God.'"

Once more the audience honored my request, but this time there was no laughter. People hugged one another and tears fell freely. I thanked everyone for the opportunity to speak, offered them God's blessing, and started to walk off the stage.

I got no more than five or six feet when Kathy Mattea stopped me and hugged me. We just stood there hugging while the Jumbotron made sure everyone could see us. The applause was deafening. She then smiled at me, let me go, and walked up to the podium to introduce the next musical performer. Her voice cracked and she said how moved she was by what the rabbi said, and the house again exploded with applause. I admit that I was tempted to walk back on stage, heal the sick, grab a guitar, and begin a new career as a Nashville star, but my handler grabbed my arm and led me back downstairs.

As I walked down the stairs, I asked myself why what I said mattered. Why was it so moving? The answer came as quickly as the question: because it was the truth. You know in your heart, you know in a way that theology can never touch, that you are one with God, the Source and Substance of all life, and thus one with all living things. And knowing who you are makes lovingkindness possible.

It is vital that you know who you are if you are to live with lovingkindness. You cannot fake lovingkindness. Authentic lovingkindness is the natural response to the simple truth of your being one with all beings in, with, and as God. You are God manifest as you. This is why the first of the Thirteen Attributes of Lovingkindness is Y-H-V-H; to remind you who you really are: God. Or as the Upanishads put it, *tat tvam assi*, Thou art That.

There is no better statement of the first attribute than this one written by the kabbalist Abraham Abulafia in the thirteenth century: "Behold you are God and God is you; for you are so intimately adhering to God that you cannot by any means be separate from God, for you are God. See now that I, even I, am God. He is I and I am He."

The kabbalist is speaking from the perspective of *mochin d'gadlut*, spacious mind, rather than *mochin d'katnut*, narrow mind. These terms come from the vocabulary of the Hasidim, the Eastern European Jewish mystics of the eighteenth century. While I am in no way suggesting a historical link between the Hasidim of Poland and the Buddhist sages of Asia, it is interesting to note that both traditions employ these terms and do so in similar ways.

Narrow mind imagines itself as separate from the world. It is isolated, often alienated, and sees the world as a zero-sum game in which its success depends on another's failure. Scarcity defines the world of *mochin d'katnut;* fear is its primary emotion and anger its most common expression.

Spacious mind, in both Judaism and Buddhism, sees the self as part of the Whole: *I am in the Father and the Father is in me.* As such, spacious mind engages life from a place of interdependence and compassion. Abundance is the hallmark of the world as *mochin d'gadlut* perceives it. As such, love rather than fear is its emotional foundation, and lovingkindness rather than anger is its defining characteristic. As we cultivate the Thirteen Attributes of Lovingkindness found in this book we continually shift from narrow mind to spacious mind. Spacious mind does not negate narrow mind, but embraces and includes it in a larger vision. In this way your sense of self is freed from fear and anger, and you are empowered to engage the world with your own unique expression of lovingkindness.

Jesus is talking about the same thing in the Gospel according to John:

> Philip said to him, "Lord, show us the Father, and we will be satisfied." Jesus said to him, "Have I been with you all this time, Philip, and you still do not know me? Whoever has seen me has seen the Father.... Believe me that I am in the Father and the Father is in me. (John 14:8–10)

In this passage, Philip sees neither the true nature of Jesus nor the true nature of himself. He still imagines God is other rather than all. The Name of God, the *yod-hey-vav-hey* that is manifest as your body, is a form of the Hebrew verb *to be*. God is not a being, or even a supreme being; God is being itself. All that was, is, and will be is God. And, since God is also called *Ayin,* the Nothing that includes all things, nonbeing and being are both God. God is what is and what isn't at each and every moment. Or, to use a term from Buddhism, God is *tathata,* Suchness, Reality—in you, around you, as you.

Philip wants Jesus to point to God, whereas Jesus knows he and we are God. "You want to look at something and call it God," Jesus is saying in effect. "Then look at me. I am in God and God is in me. God is all of me, though I am not all of God. Just as the ocean is all of the wave and yet the wave is not all of the ocean, so you and I and all things are God, just not all of God."

This is what it means to be the image of God. But not yet the likeness. Jesus is trying to teach Philip, and through Philip, each of us, that to know you are God is not enough; you have to act godly as well. This is why the second of the Thirteen Attributes is also Y-H-V-H, to remind you that everything else is God as well.

When we see the world as Philip did, when we see the world from the perspective of narrow mind, we see diversity without unity. We might have an inkling that we are God, but we have no idea that the other is God as well. Things appear discrete, independent, and competing. The world seems dominated by the idea of "looking out for number one." Living is "dog eat dog." Success is a zero-sum game: If I am to win, then you must lose.

When we see the world as Jesus did, however, when we see the world from the perspective of spacious mind, we see a greater unity embracing and transcending diversity. The world is integral and interdependent. Looking out for number one is only possible when we look out for numbers two, three, and four as well. Hence the *bodhisattva* vow, "Though sentient beings are innumerable, I vow to save them all."

There is nothing wrong with narrow mind. It, too, is a manifestation of God, and a necessary one at that. As Jesus' rabbinic contemporary, Hillel, said some two millennia ago, "If I am not for myself, who will be for me?" Narrow mind is all about being for yourself. The problem arises only when taking care of yourself is done at the expense of others.

Spacious mind speaks to the second half of Hillel's aphorism, "If I am only for myself, what am I?" Without spacious mind, you are fearful, anxious, alienated, and alone.

Spacious mind offers a different view: *See now that I, even I, am God. God is I and I am God.* It is to spacious mind that God speaks, saying, "Be holy, as I, God, am holy" (Leviticus 19:2). Before we can behave in a holy manner, however, we first have to see ourselves as holy. Unless and until we understand our true nature, we cannot act from that nature. As long as we are locked in narrow mind and cannot experience others and ourselves from the perspective of spacious mind, we can get nowhere.

The purpose of the first two attributes, the repetition of Y-H-V-H, is to awaken us to the innate and intrinsic holiness of all things. If God is all, God is also me and you.

BECOMING WHO YOU ARE: VISUALIZING GOD AS SELF AND OTHER

One way to practice this is with the visualization using the tetragrammaton, the four-letter Name of God, the יהוה I taught at the tsunami relief concert. Visualize the Name vertically:

י

ה

ו

ה

The *yod* (Y) is your head and face; the *hey* (H) is your shoulders and arms; the *vav* (V) is your torso; and the final *hey* (H) is your pelvis and legs. Visualize this when lying down to sleep at night, and before getting out of bed in the morning. See yourself as the Name of God, the Image of God. Once this practice takes hold, it is very difficult to shake the awesome responsibility that comes with it.

Not too long ago I was teaching this visualization at an interfaith teenage leadership camp in central Tennessee. I asked the kids, who ranged in age from sixteen to nineteen, to show me how they walk during the day. I had them walk up and down the room and began to point out what I saw. Most of them were slouched, their eyes locked onto the floor. We went through the Name of God visualization exercise and I asked them to walk again, this time as an incarnation of the Divine.

Most of them walked with a sense of newfound grace, their bodies straight but not stiff, the eyes meeting the eyes of their fellow campers. But some walked as royalty, impervious to the needs and presence of others. This is the difference between knowing you are God and pretending you are God. Those who know are at ease with themselves and others. Those who pretend become pompous prigs.

I mentioned this, saying, "It is not enough to know you are God, to see the Name of God written with your body. You must also see the Name in everyone and everything else. There is a Jewish legend that says each of us has an angel who walks before us calling out, 'Behold the Image and Likeness of God.' You must honor your own angel and hear everyone else's angel as well. You must see yourself and the world as God manifest in time and space. And when you do, you will naturally engage life with grace, humor, and lovingkindness."

Real holiness is effortless. It is what the Taoists call *wu wei*, acting without coercion. You don't try to be kind or patient, you simply are kind and patient. Because you don't work at it, you take no credit for it. It is a gift. You receive it and share it.

I use this exercise during my daily prayer-walk. I begin with the chanting of the Thirteen Attributes to awaken myself to the

presence of God in, with, and as all reality. I visualize myself as
Y-H-V-H, hearing my angel reminding me of my true nature as
God manifest. Then I open myself a bit wider and see everything
else as a manifestation as well. The trees, the crows, the squirrels,
everything I meet, animate and inanimate, I see and experience
as God.

At the least, I find myself feeling a great connection with all
beings. Sometimes this connection is far more intense. The trees
ask to be hugged; the sky embraces me; I find myself in conversation with birds, deer, dogs, and squirrels. While there are few
people out walking at the same time, those I do meet seem to
glow with the Name of God. I find myself spontaneously singing
out Names of God in Hebrew, Greek, Arabic, and Sanskrit. It is
an erotic kind of encounter with the world; I have this sense of
loving and being loved by the entire world. Sometimes the love
is so intense I can't walk, and simply whirl like a dervish, my
arms extended to hug the world. Sometimes I cry with joy. I do
not equate any of this with mystical experience, or, God forbid,
enlightenment. This is simply a palpable encounter with God in
and as all things.

Practice these two visualization exercises daily. Wake up
each morning and stand in front of a mirror, seeing your body as
the incarnate Name of God. As you go about your day, see everyone and everything as the Name as well. Listen for your angel
announcing your true nature, and listen for the angels of others
doing the same. In time you will break up the hard-packed soil
of narrow mind and plant in it the seeds of lovingkindness that
will soon grow and awaken in you the spacious mind that is your
holy and most true self.

GOD AS CREATIVE FORCE

Cultivating Creativity

The intuitive mind is a sacred gift and the rational
mind is a faithful servant. We have created a society
that honors the servant and has forgotten the gift.
                                                    —*Albert Einstein*

The Third Attribute of Lovingkindness is *El,* God as creative force. True creativity "flows through the human heart … from the Divine heart," says Matthew Fox in *Creativity*.[1] Among the Ninety-Nine Most Beautiful Names of God found in Islam are many that make clear God's relationship to creativity: *Al-Musawwir* (the Fashioner); *Al-Bari* (the Maker); *Al-Khaliq* (the Creator); and *Al-Badi* (the Originator). Thomas Aquinas calls God the Artist of Artists. Meister Eckhart speaks of God as "pure generation" and the "life of all things." Hildegard of Bingen writes, "God's word is in all creation, visible and invisible. The Word is living, being, spirit, all verdant greening, all creativity. The Word manifests in every creature."[2] Creativity is the way God is you in time and space. It is the way you are godly as well.

Let me be very clear: By creativity I am not talking about being able to draw, paint, write, dance, or any other activity. Lots of people can do these things very well without ever tapping into creativity. The creativity I am talking about, the creativity that is essential to lovingkindness, is the realization that you in and of yourself are a creative act. Why is this realization necessary for the practice of lovingkindness? Because realizing your own creativity takes you out of the past, out of the known, beyond the labels of gender, race, nationality, ethnicity, religion, and the like. Creativity is the breaking down of all you know so that the new, the unknown, may emerge. And the experience of that breaking down is essential to lovingkindness because it allows you to engage the moment—and everyone and everything in it—fresh, without the baggage of the past.

Unless and until you can tap into creativity, you cannot engage the world with lovingkindness. You can fake it, you can act in ways that appear loving and kind, but your actions are always tainted by the drive for self-preservation. You will experience creativity not as a gift but as an achievement. You will feel inflated rather than humbled. You will feel important, and you will want to be seen by others as important. And this makes lovingkindness impossible.

Creativity, then, is a paradoxical phenomenon, because it relies on your own uniqueness while at the same time eliminating the ego that knows itself to be unique. The paradox is resolved, however, in the creative engagement with life. In this act of creative engagement, narrow egoic mind—the mind that equates uniqueness with separateness and superiority—gives way to the spacious mind, which recognizes that your uniqueness is matched by the uniqueness of everything else.

Martin Buber, one of the greatest sages of the twentieth century, wrote, "Every person born into this world represents something new, something that never existed before, something original and unique."[3] You are a totally original and unique manifestation of God, but you are not the only such manifestation of God. If you imitate others, you are denying your own originality. If you force others to imitate you, their originality—

their integrity—is compromised. Rather, you have to make room for originality in its almost infinite diversity.

Realizing *El* is, to paraphrase Buber, to know and recognize that you are unique in the world in your particular character. In grasping this concept, you understand that there has never been anyone like you before, for if there were, there would be no need for you to be in the world. Every single thing is a new thing in the world and is called upon to fulfill its particularity in this world. "For verily: that this is not done, is the reason why the coming of the Messiah is delayed. Every man's foremost task is the actualization of his unique unprecedented and never-recurring potentialities, and not the repetition of something that another, and be it even the greatest, has already achieved."[4]

According to Buber, it is the lack of personal creativity that keeps the messianic age from unfolding. Why? Because without creativity, and the personal authenticity that comes with it, lovingkindness—the hallmark of the messianic age—is impossible. If you engage the world from a fixed model rooted in the past, you live by imitation. You undermine your own sense of purpose. While you may avoid doing bad, and may even do some good, the gift of your full potential will never actualize.

The noted rabbinic sage Zusya says, "In the world to come I shall not be asked why I was not like Moses. I shall be asked why I was not myself." To be yourself is to actualize your creativity. It is to engage the world in a way uniquely your own.

Two thousand years ago, the Rabbis compared the minting of Roman coins to the creation of human beings. Every emperor would have coins issued with his likeness on them. Each coin bore the identical face of the emperor; they were uniform and interchangeable. God, the Rabbis taught, did things differently. While each human is "minted" in the image and likeness of God, no two people bear the same face, and no one face is the Face of God. God is multifaceted, and yours is one of those facets. To honor your true identity as God, you must be true to your own face.

CULTIVATING LOVINGKINDNESS THROUGH CREATIVITY

The book of Genesis reveals this to us in God's call to Abram: *Go forth* [lech lecha] *from your land, from your nation, from your parents' house and go to the land I will show you* (Genesis 12:1). The Hebrew *lech lecha,* usually translated as "Go forth!" actually means: "Walk toward your self!" While standard translations of the Bible make it clear that God wants Abram to go somewhere in time and space, the text itself is more ambiguous and interesting.

As I read the Torah, God is saying to Abram, and through Abram to each of us as well, that we are to turn inward and free ourselves from the conditioning of narrow mind—the conditioning of nationality, tribe, culture, religion, parental influence—and see the world as God wishes us to see it: with spacious mind, with a creativity that is uniquely our own.

There are few passages in any scripture as radical as this. If you think that the call to creativity is Abram's alone, then the Torah is irrelevant to you here. But if you realize that Abram represents each of us, if you realize that God is calling to you here and now to free yourself of all conditioning and embrace life unfettered by habituated norms imposed upon you by religion, society, culture, and parents, then you will find in this call a challenge that threatens everything you think you know about who you are and what you are to do. This is the spiritual challenge of Jesus:

> If you bring forth that which is within you, that which is within you will save you. If you do not bring forth that which is within you, that which is within you will destroy you.[5]

What is "within you" is your unique creative face. When you bring out this face—that is, when you see the world with spacious mind—you will see it as the manifestation of God's ongoing creativity. This is what Jesus calls the Kingdom of God: "His disciples said to him, 'When will the Kingdom come?' [Jesus said,] 'It will not come by watching for it. They will not say, "Look, it is here!" or "Look, it is there!" Rather the Kingdom of the Father is spread out upon the earth, but people do not see it.'"[6]

When you do see it, you will understand what Jesus means when he says, "I am the light that is over all things. I am all. From me all come forth, and to me all extends. Split a piece of wood, and I am there. Lift up the stone, and you will find me there."[7] This is the same as Abraham Abulafia's "Behold I am He and He is me."

Creativity, then, is seeing and interacting with life without the prism of conditioning, seeing the divine qualities in life, as God sees things, and yet seeing them as unique and special unto themselves. Like snowflakes, no two of which are alike, and the snow they comprise and that we perceive as a singular entity, we see the unity and diversity in a greater nonduality. This is what Krishna wishes his disciple Arjuna to see in the Hindu *Bhagavad Gita* (11:6–7):

> Arjuna, see all the universe animate and inanimate, and whatever else you wish to see; all stands here as one in my body.... [And Arjuna looked and] Everywhere was boundless divinity containing all astonishing things.

When we step out of fixed and narrow mind, we see all things as astonishing. We know that God is all and engage life from a place of effortless creativity that gives rise to effortless lovingkindness.

How do you manifest this creativity? By practicing *lech lecha,* inward journeying, or meditation. "Meditation is a way of putting aside altogether everything that man has conceived of himself and of the world. So he has a totally different kind of mind,"[8] said Krishnamurti, one of the twentieth century's greatest philosophers.

You must look inward to see whether you are engaging the world from the narrow conditioned mind or from the spacious and unconditioned mind. What you do is look. Just look. When you see that you are coming from narrow mind, simply be aware of this fact. That awareness alone will free you from the conditioning. Do not think that your responses to each moment are automatic and instantaneous. They may be grounded in habit, but there is always a moment between an action and your reaction to it in which to look and see if you are acting from conditioning or creativity. What are the signs?

If you are coming from narrow, conditioned, and clever mind, you will find yourself experiencing anxiety and fear. If you are coming from spacious, unconditioned, and creative mind, you will experience tranquility and compassion. It is that simple. But you do have to look.

MANIFESTING CREATIVITY THROUGH MINDFULNESS MEDITATION

While there are many ways of looking at the mind, one of the best is mindfulness meditation taught by various schools of Buddhism.

Sit solidly cross-legged on a cushion on the floor or in a chair with your feel flat on the floor. Sit relaxed, but upright, with your back naturally curved, not stiff or bent. Rest your hands on your thighs, palms up or down. Tuck your chin in slightly so that you imagine a string pulling you up from the base of your spine through the top of your head. Rest your eyes downward, fixed four to six feet in front of you. Soften your gaze, and keep your eyes open. It may take some time to get used to this way of sitting, and if you need to move a bit during meditation to maintain comfort, do so gently.

Once you are sitting properly, shift your attention to your breath. All meditation practices take note of the breath. It is, as Genesis says, the way God breathes consciousness into us. Don't control the breath, simply pay attention to it. Breathe through your nose and be mindful of the breath as it enters and leaves your nostrils.

It sounds simple, and it is; simple, but not easy. What makes it difficult is that narrow mind cannot abide mindfulness and tosses out thoughts and feelings like clay skeet targets for you to shoot at. You cannot stop the machine from tossing the skeet— just don't lift the rifle and shoot at them. Notice the fact that you are thinking or feeling and return your attention to your breath.

When you realize how the mind works, spinning thoughts and tossing them into awareness, you realize how conditioned this way of thinking is. You realize that the mind is not creative as much as it is chaotic. The creativity comes when you are no longer knocked over by the chaos. Not being knocked over is what the Tibetan master Sakyong Rinpoche calls "holding your seat." It is allowing chaos to be chaos without losing your sense of humor and dignity. I call it becoming a Weeble.

Weebles are weighted, egg-shaped toys. Weebles, as their ads claimed in the 1970s, "wobble but they don't fall down." I know that my Zen master Sasaki Roshi had little tolerance for wobbling. As the Zen proverb goes, "When hungry, eat; when tired, sleep; But above all don't wobble." I wobble, but like a Weeble I manage to come back to center without falling over. If you can live well without wobbling, fine. If you wobble, fine, too. Just don't fall over.

Mindfulness meditation is Weeble practice. You watch in amazement as narrow mind spins one wild thought after another, hoping to catch you in its drama and knock you to the mat. The more you learn to watch this process during meditation, the more you will be able to watch it during the rest of your day. Watching the chaos frees you from it.

As you learn how to recognize the chaos and not be bowled over by it, you can hold your seat and allow creativity to manifest in you. Creativity in this sense is your ability to engage the moment with *wu wei,* noncoercive action. You do not react from habit, but can meet the moment fresh. Notice that meditation does not erase the habits of heart and mind; rather, it allows you to see them for the habits they are, enabling you get some distance from them in order to choose the right way—rather than the rote way—to be in that moment.

FEARLESS COMPASSION

Harvesting Kindness through Compassionate Honesty

*A religious man is a person who holds God and man
in one thought at one time, at all times, who suffers
harm done to others, whose greatest passion is compassion, whose greatest strength is love and defiance of
despair.*

—*Abraham Joshua Heschel*

Compassion isn't "mealy-mouthed piety," says Marc Ian Barasch
in *Field Notes on the Compassionate Life*;[1] rather, it is a coura-
geous stand against nihilism. When the Dalai Lama says, "My
only religion is kindness," and Pope John Paul II calls for a
"civilization of love," they are urging us to transform human
consciousness. I agree: Compassion of this sort depends on and
flows directly from your realization of the true nature of self and
other as God, and your capacity to creatively engage both, free
from the prejudices of the past. The first three Attributes of
Lovingkindness prepare the ground for compassion, but you
must still harvest it yourself.

What is it about lovingkindness that makes it a power unto
itself, a power capable of "transmuting even the most relentless
enmity,"[2] and changing an enemy into a friend? Can it be that

"being nice" to someone is enough to change them and their relationship with you? I don't think so.

I don't think lovingkindness is about being nice. I believe it is about being fearless. When the Dalai Lama affirms the religion of kindness, he is talking about a religious attitude that mirrors the truth without distortion. The greatest kindness one can offer another is compassionate honesty. That is to say, to allow the other to see the consequences of her actions without imposing any judgments or prejudices of your own. It is this seeing that transforms the seer.

You cannot change another person, and if you think you can and intend to use lovingkindness as a strategy for doing so, you will fail—and fail miserably. Indeed, you cannot even change yourself, for the you that is to be changed is the you that is instigating the change. This is like trying to hear your own ear or kiss your own lips. It can't be done.

What changes us is our encounter with reality. When we really see what it is we do and how what we do impacts the world around us, then we are ready to change, if change is necessary. I have learned this over and over again—I have to learn this over and over again, since in my case the lesson doesn't seem to translate from event to event.

I have what might be called a pleaser personality. I want to please other people not because I care about them, but because by pleasing them I can keep them under control. Or so I tell myself. I tend to agree to things I really don't want to do just to keep the peace. Of course the peace this keeps isn't real; in fact, I experience resentment and anger rather than a sense of peace when I do this. Yet I do it over and over again, thinking that I am getting away with something, and that people can't see through what I am doing.

The truth is just the opposite. People who know me well will call me on this behavior. They will show me that it hurts them to have me try to manipulate them by playing the pleaser.

When they are clear with me about the impact of my actions, simply stating the truth without attacking me in the process, I cannot help but realize that there is no love in what I do. In fact, my behavior is driven by fear: fear of their reaction if I were honest and simply said "no" to the request at hand.

By showing me the truth without using that truth to manipulate me, my friends and family have freed me to respond to situations in a new way. I hesitate to even call this "change." I don't know if anything has changed. All I know is that I see and exercise options that were unknown to me previously. This is how compassion transforms relationships—not by changing anything but by revealing everything.

Can you live this fearless compassion? I don't know. I would like to believe so, but I cannot point to anyone I know who does so constantly. Perhaps compassion is not an end but a process; you don't master it, you simply work with it day by day. What would it be like to work with compassion?

My own experience with this suggests that it is like watching a drama on television. In order to engage the viewer, the actors must make their emotions crystal clear. When they do so, they spark something in me that engages with them. Their feelings trigger feelings of my own. Once this happens, I am hooked and will watch the show from beginning to end. If the show is well scripted and well acted, I will feel a certain sympathy with the characters, sharing their feelings to some extent. Yet all the while I know that I am watching television. I know that when the show ends, so will my engagement with the characters and their lives. I can watch and allow myself to become emotionally engaged without ever forgetting that what I am watching has nothing to do with my life.

There is empathy and objectivity at the same time. I am startled when the actors are startled; angered when they are angered; fearful for them when they appear fearful for themselves. And I can get a cup of tea during a commercial without dragging those feelings with me from the den to the kitchen. I am fully engaged and yet in no way entrapped. That is what compassion does for me as well.

When I am compassionate toward myself and others, I am free to be fully engaged in what is happening with them and between them and myself. I can allow for all the feelings that the situation conjures, and yet I am not trapped by the feelings or the situation. I am a mirror on which the emotions of the moment play out, but when the moment passes, the mirror retains nothing. This is true compassion: reflecting all and retaining none.

This may seem odd to you. The word *compassion* comes from the Latin for "shared" *(com)* "suffering" *(passion),* and you may think of compassion as sharing another's pain. But of what value is that to you or the other? If I come to you in pain and you end up with the same pain, all we have done is add to the world's suffering. We have done nothing to alleviate it. I want you to understand my pain, to respond to it deeply, but not to take it on yourself. I want you to help me see what you see and what I cannot see. I want you to engage my pain as if I were an actor in a drama you were watching. Mirror my experience, but don't embrace it as your own.

To have the courage to mirror reality, you have to be willing to feel everything even as you cling to nothing. Again, this is like watching an engaging television show or film. The point of going to a horror movie is to be scared. If you can't let yourself feel fear, the movie is boring. If you can't separate the fear generated by the movie from your life outside the movie theater, you are lost in a false reality. You want to be open to fear but not trapped by fear. And not just fear, but love, hate, joy, anguish, anger, repentance, guilt, ecstasy—the entire gamut of human emotions.

When you are open to all feelings, you realize that you feel all that another feels. A whole heart is a heart open to and welcoming of the full range of human emotion. This does not mean that you are free to act on your feelings. It only means that you are free to feel them, and when you do so, you have compassion for neighbor and stranger alike, for you know their heart as your own. In Judaism this knowing without limits is called the compassion of God, and, since you are God manifest in your time and place, this compassion is potentially yours as well.

When the daughters of Zelophehad (in Numbers 27:1–12) heard that their father's land was being divided among men to the exclusion of women, they assembled to take counsel. They said, "The compassion of God is not like the compassion of men. The compassion of men extends more to men than to women, whereas the compassion of God extends equally to men and women and to all: 'The Lord is good to all, and His mercies are over all His worlds'" (Psalm 145:9) [*Sifre Numbers, Pinchas*]. The sisters complained of this injustice to Moses, who took their case to God, who settled the matter in their favor, allowing them to inherit their father's lands.

God's compassion extends to all creatures, sentient and non-sentient, animate and inanimate. God's love is *ahavah rabbah,* infinite and unbounded. It cannot be earned and it cannot be lost. But it can be ignored.

You might think that accepting God's compassion would be easy and something everyone would clamor for. The opposite is often the case. There is something about so many of us that wants to be blamed, that wants to feel unworthy of God's love. In this way we maintain the drama of narrow mind through a false humility.

Claiming to be unworthy of God's compassion is not an act of self-emptying, but of self-aggrandizement. It is not an act of humility, but of narcissism. You are saying, in effect, "While others may be loved by God, I am different from them. My sins are greater than theirs. I am too lost even for God to find me." This outward expression of despair is in fact done with a wink and a nod: "Look at me! I alone among all who live am too wicked for

God! And if I am too wicked to receive compassion, I am certainly too wicked to act compassionately."

As odd as it may sound, many of us actually wear our sins as badges of honor. Not that we would admit this to others or even to ourselves, but if we look honestly enough, pride surrounds the drama of our evil. This is why so much of religion, any religion, focuses on God's judgment and punishment rather than on forgiveness and love. This is why the Thirteen Attributes, which do not include judgment at all, are so powerful and subversive to the maintenance of the narrow mind.

CULTIVATING COMPASSION THROUGH *METTA* PRACTICE

One of the most powerful ways I know to cultivate compassion is through the Buddhist practice of *metta,* lovingkindness. *Metta* is a Pali word with two meanings: "gentle" and "friend." *Metta* practice is a way of gently befriending both narrow mind and the fearful notion of self and other that arises from it. The Buddhist teacher Sharon Salzberg is my primary source for *metta* practice. She teaches that "Buddha described a true friend as being a helper, someone who will protect us when we are unable to take care of ourselves, who will be a refuge to us when we are afraid."[3] *Metta* practice can be that friend to you.

Metta is compassion freed from compulsion; it is the ability to open to what is without the need to change it. This is true most powerfully when applied to our own inner states. When we look at ourselves as we might watch a film, we see much that we do not like. Our initial response might be to deny what we see, or to jump in and try to change it into something we do like. Neither denial nor desire to change are effective in this case. The first simply allows the negative to continue unabated, and the second only makes it harder to change by violently seeking to change it. *Metta* offers a third alternative: Embrace with compassion. As Sharon Salzberg writes:

We can open to everything with the healing force of love. When we feel love, our mind is expansive and open enough to include the entirety of life in full awareness, both its pleasures and its pains. We feel neither betrayed by pain nor overcome by it, and thus we can contact that which is undamaged within us regardless of the situation. *Metta* sees truly that our integrity is inviolate, no matter what our life situation may be. We do not need to fear anything. We are whole: our deepest happiness is intrinsic to the nature of our minds, and it is not damaged through uncertainty and change.[4]

Metta practice consists of repeating a series of affirmations, and doing so with a fully attentive and focused mind. Two of the leading lights in North American Buddhism, Sharon Salzberg and Pema Chödrön, both of whom have been my teachers, offer detailed instruction in *metta* practice, and I recommend that you read any of their fine books on the subject. What I want to share with you here is how I practice *metta,* in the hope that this will jump-start your own exploration into its life-altering potential and encourage you to read more about it on your own.

Metta practice is essentially the act of wishing self and others well. But it is more than a psychological game, or the fierce focus on empty affirmations. I am reminded of the *Seinfeld* episode called "Serenity Now," in which George's father is trying to gain some equanimity in his life by chanting (and, more often than not, screaming), "Serenity now! Serenity now!" Needless to say, it didn't work, and it made for some very funny television.

I know people who think of *metta* practice as a solemn Serenity Now exercise. But these are people who have not done it at all, or at least not deeply enough. The affirmations used in *metta* practice set your intention. When you ask to become free from fear, you are planting the seeds of fearlessness in your mind and heart. You are not conjuring fearlessness, but rather turning the rudder of your life toward fearlessness. Just as the slightest turn can, in time, change the course of a boat, so the intention of *metta* can turn the course of your life.

One example from my own life may illustrate this. I was once struggling with my relationship with my father. It had gotten to the point where I could not talk to him on the telephone, let alone face-to-face, without shutting down. It was a fear reaction engendered by what I saw as his disappointment in my life choices. Because he seemed to disapprove of who I was and what I did, I became angry and defensive. Rather than talk this out with him, I let it stew until I could barely talk with him at all. I don't know if he was aware of this, but that is how I felt.

A therapist urged me to confront my feelings and then my dad. I could do the former but not the latter. A Buddhist friend introduced me to *metta* practice, and I began to spend time visualizing my dad sitting in front of me and consciously wishing him to be well and at peace. I did this for a few minutes each day for several weeks. I didn't really feel it was making any difference.

Then one day I called home. Usually I called when I knew my mother would answer the phone. We would talk at length, and then she would hand the phone to my father for a quick "How are you" and then he would hand it back to my mother so we could say good-bye. This time, however, she was out and my dad answered. We started into the same perfunctory exchange and were about to hang up. Just before I did, however, I said, "I love you, Dad." Without missing a beat he replied in kind.

Something shifted. I felt a physical change in my body, not simply a relaxation of tension, though there was that, but a turning of my heart. I really have no words for this. But from that time on, and it has been years now, my father and I speak lovingly to one another. And now that my mother is nearly deaf and no longer able to talk on the phone for any length of time, my dad and I have the long conversations. I credit this shift to *metta* practice.

I practice *metta* on myself, on friends, on loved ones, and on people with whom I am in conflict. When dealing with myself and those I love, I use photographs to help focus my attention. I will share a self-focused *metta* practice with you as a model. Because of its length, I do this version of *metta* on special occasions, such as my birthday or at times when I am feeling truly lost or stuck. I am sharing it here to give you something to work with as you create your own *metta* practice.

I begin with a photo of myself when I was six. Knowing that this child still resides in me, bringing with him both playfulness and foolishness, I want to make peace with this inner child. I say to the inner child through the photograph:

> May you be free from fear.
> May you be free from compulsion.
> May you be blessed with love.
> May you be blessed with peace.

When the inner child is free from fear, it is free to play rather than scheme. When it is free from compulsion, it is free to create rather than imitate. When the inner child is blessed with love, it is loving and unafraid. When the inner child is at peace, it is capable of engaging the moment with spontaneity and freshness. What is true of my inner child is true of all my inner states, and of all those people with whom I practice *metta* as well: When we are free, we are fearless and creative.

I then move on to a picture of me in my twenties, knowing that this "me" had dreams that are still unrealized, and unrealizable, given the choices I have made in my life. To this self I say the same thing:

> May you be free from fear.
> May you be free from compulsion.
> May you be blessed with love.
> May you be blessed with peace.

I continue this practice with photographs of myself at different stages of my life, welcoming these selves and wishing them well. What I find as I do this is that I can make peace with choices I have made, and the dreams these choices have both fostered and killed. I close this *metta* session with the following:

> May I be free from fear.
> May I be free from compulsion.
> May I be blessed with love.
> May I be blessed with peace.

I then sit for a few minutes in silence, closing the session with the Prayer of St. Francis of Assisi:

> Lord, make me an instrument of your peace.
> Where there is hatred, let me sow love;
> Where there is injury, pardon;
> Where there is doubt, faith;
> Where there is despair, hope;
> Where there is darkness, light;
> Where there is sadness, joy.
> O Divine Master,
> Grant that I may not so much seek
> To be consoled, as to console,
> To be understood, as to understand,
> To be loved, as to love,
> For it is in giving that we receive;
> It is in pardoning that we are pardoned;
> It is in dying that we are born to eternal life.

I also use photographs when doing *metta* with loved ones. I prop the photo up in front of me and offer the blessing three times for each person I am working with:

May [the person's name] be free from fear.

May [the person's name] be free from compulsion.

May [the person's name] be blessed with love.

May [the person's name] be blessed with peace.

If photographs are not available, as is often the case when I am dealing with a person about whom I have strong negative feelings, I do my best to imagine the person sitting across from me as I offer her the same four blessings.

However you engage in *metta* practice, I suggest that you close your session with the *Discourse on Good Will* from the *Sutta Nipata* of the Buddha. This highly truncated version is my own, but you can find a fuller and more standard translation by Stephen Ruppenthal in Eknath Easwaran's wonderful anthology *God Makes the Rivers to Flow*.

May all who live be filled with lasting joy.

May deception end, and delusion cease.

May no one despise another, nor wish them ill.

May love grow boundless, and may hatred end with the
    release of fear.[5]

Among the promised benefits of *metta* practice are an easier night's sleep, a glowing countenance, the protection and love of celestial beings, and rebirth in happier worlds. I haven't found any of this to be true in my case. What I have found when I make time to engage in *metta* practice is a spaciousness of heart that allows me to be at peace with reality. Yes, I struggle with aspects of myself and certainly with others, but through *metta* I regain the awareness of our shared womb, our shared suffering, our shared quest for happiness, and I realize that things are as they are because they cannot be other than they are at this moment. Accepting reality with compassion allows me to engage it with equanimity, and move on.

This is why compassion is the Fourth Attribute of Lovingkindness. Without the ability to see what is and not become trapped in it, without the capacity to engage it with an open and loving heart, without the courage to be present to the world, you cannot act with lovingkindness. If you are trapped in your own feelings, you will only act in ways that perpetuate those feelings, whether or not they are helpful. If your heart is closed and fearful, you will flee from reality into fantasy and your dealings with the world will be false and shallow. If you are not present to reality, you are incapable of effective, creative, and loving action. You are like a filmgoer who cannot let the movie cease when the show is over. You live in a drama of your own making. It is real to you, and irrelevant to the world. Compassion returns you to the world, and lovingkindness allows you to engage it fully and well.

ENGAGING LIFE
THROUGH GRACE

Being Present in the Moment

*God, give us grace to accept with serenity the things
that cannot be changed, courage to change the things
that should be changed, and the wisdom to distinguish
the one from the other.*

—Reinhold Niebuhr

As we saw in the previous chapter, compassion, the fourth of the
Thirteen Attributes of Lovingkindness, is the capacity to open to
life as it is without trying to make it other than it is. Grace, the
fifth attribute, is the ability to engage life as it is without wishing
it were other than it is. Compassion reveals the stage on which
life is to be played out; grace is the play itself.

The master of grace is Job. Job is an innocent man of faith,
a true believer, whom God gives over to the torment of Satan in
order to test just how deep Job's faith goes. Job's children die, he
loses his wealth, and his body erupts in painful, oozing sores. He
is reduced to sitting in the rubble of his life, scratching his sores
with a broken shard of pottery. His wife urges him to "curse God
and die like a man" (Job 2:9), and his friends come to comfort

him by trying to get him to confess to some secret crime for which he is now being punished.

Job tells his wife that we have no right to accept only the good from God and must learn to endure the horrible as well. His friends argue that God is just and nothing bad can happen to you if you do not do something evil to incur the wrath of God. Job denies doing anything wrong and demands that God show up and explain these divine actions.

God does show up, but does not explain the actions at all. Instead, God makes it very clear that all human notions about right and wrong, good and evil, justice and injustice are just that—human notions. God is beyond all that. God is what is, and to expect God to comply with human theological speculation is ludicrous.

In the end Job realizes the truth of this assertion, and falls silent. We should do the same. Only when our stories fall silent, only when we stop insisting that God fit into the neat boxes of our self-serving and self-aggrandizing theologies, are we able to engage reality as it is. And engaging reality as it is—this is real grace.

What does grace have to do with lovingkindness? As long as you think God is about reward and punishment, you will, as Job's friends did, blame the victim. Blaming the victim may exonerate your idea of God from the charge of immorality, but at the same time it makes authentic lovingkindness impossible. Blaming the victim allows for pity, sympathy, even empathy, but not lovingkindness.

You may even say to yourself, "There but for the grace of God go I," but in your heart you will know it is more about the "I" than about God. Somewhere in the recesses of your mind lurks the notion that people get what they deserve, for if they don't, the world is fundamentally unjust, and that is a viewpoint most of us cannot abide.

What Job discovers is that the world is simply the world; that human ideas of justice and fairness have nothing to do with it; that God is the wild whirlwind spinning out a wild drama of order and chaos without you in mind at all. God's grace is in spinning the drama; your grace is in learning to engage it without being blown away by it.

Grace is to life as current is to ocean. Grace is the dynamic nature of things. It is the flow, the dance, the turning of the universe. Without grace nothing happens, for grace is what happens. Hence the prophet Isaiah taught that God's throne is founded in grace (Isaiah 16:5). The Rabbis agreed: "From the beginning the earth was built only upon grace" (*Mekilta*, Vol. II, p. 69).

To be in touch with the world at its most true, is to be graceful, literally filled with grace. This is what the Rabbis taught when they said, "To an earthly king one goes full and returns empty. To God one goes empty and returns full" (*Pesikta Rabbatai*, 185a).

Going empty into God is the key to finding and embodying grace. During one of my Sabbath visits to my early teacher Rabbi Reuven at his kabbalistic kibbutz in Israel, I passed the rabbi on the sidewalk leading into the dining hall. I was carrying several books, and as we passed one another, he slapped the books out of my hands and shouted, "No carrying on Shabbos!" *Shabbos* is the Yiddish word for "Sabbath."

"But Rabbi," I stuttered, "there is an *eruv* around the kibbutz. Carrying is allowed in here." An *eruv* is a boundary placed around a space that defines what is inside that space as "home" and thus allows you to carry items between buildings as you can between rooms of a house.

Reuven waited until I had picked up the books. "Yes, we have an *eruv,* you are right," and then without any hint of what was coming he slapped the books out of my hands once again, shouting, "No carrying on Shabbos!" I stared at him dumbly.

"No carrying on Shabbos," he repeated flatly.

"Yes," I said, looking at the books lying on the sidewalk. "No carrying on Shabbos. So I am not carrying anything."

"Drop it!"

"Drop what?!"

Then he grabbed me in a playful hammerlock, and rapped me on my head with his knuckles. After a few bangs he stopped knocking, kissed me on the head and let me go, saying, "The head, Rami, drop the head. Your head is full of ideas, words, schemes, notions, theories, teachings from this rabbi and that rabbi; your head is so heavy it is a wonder you can even balance it on your neck. You carry all this baggage, but not on Shabbos. No carrying on Shabbos." Reuven bent down, picked up the books, kissing each in turn, handed them to me, and walked away.

Shabbos, as Rabbi Reuven was trying to teach me, is living in harmony with spacious mind. Living in harmony with spacious mind is living without fear, and thus without anger, greed, and worry. It is living in grace. There is nothing I lack on Shabbos, nothing I need to know that I don't already know. On Shabbos I was to put down the burden of learning and just know. This is the new covenant that God reveals through the prophet Jeremiah:

> Days are coming when I will seal a new covenant with you. It will be a different covenant than that which I made with your ancestors.... This is the covenant I will make with you: I shall place My Torah within you; I will write My Teaching on your heart; then I will be your God and you will be My child. Then you will no longer need teachers and sages urging you to know Me, for you shall know Me naturally; from the smallest among you to the greatest, all will know Me. And I will forgive you all your errors, and let fade all memory of your wickedness. (Jeremiah 31:31–34)

The Sabbath is a taste of this new covenant, a compact rooted in knowing from within rather than learning from without. Knowing from within and living in harmony with that knowing is living gracefully.

While invented by the Jews and strictly regulated by Jewish law for observant Jews, the practice of Sabbath-making is for everyone. I am not talking about going to synagogue on Saturdays, mosque on Fridays, or church on Sundays. I am talking about setting aside time each week to live without carrying, to put down all you know; to set aside your story and live from what remains. To make Shabbos this way requires no effort, but a great deal of trust.

When the Hebrews wandered in the desert God fed them with manna (Exodus 16:31). Each day they walked out into the wilderness to gather all they could eat for that day. But nothing was to be kept over to the next day. The only exception to this rule was collecting manna on Friday, when two-days' worth of manna could be collected so that the people would have something to eat on the Sabbath when no fresh manna was delivered. Those who tried to hoard manna on other days found the leftovers rotted and maggot-filled. You could share what you have but you could not cling to what you have.

This is the key to grace. Each day God provides you with exactly what you need for that day. If you take of it freely, and embody it fully, then all is well. If you seek more than you can eat in hopes of stockpiling it for the future, what you hoard rots. Today is for today only. Tomorrow will take care of itself. Jesus makes this idea central to his message:

> Therefore, I tell you, do not worry about your life, what you will eat or what you will drink, nor about your body, what you will wear. Is not life more than food, and the body more than clothing? Look at the birds of the air; they neither sow nor reap nor gather into barns, and yet

your heavenly Father feeds them. Are you not of more value than they? And can your worrying add a single hour to your span of life?

And why do you worry about clothing? Consider the lilies of the field, how they grow; they neither toil nor spin; yet I tell you, even Solomon in all his glory was not clothed like one of these. But if God so clothes the grass of the field, which is alive today and tomorrow is thrown into the oven, will He not much more clothe you—you of little faith? Therefore, do not worry, saying, "What shall we eat?" or "What shall we drink?" or "What shall we wear?" For it is the Gentiles who strive for all these things; and indeed your heavenly Father knows that you need all these things. But strive first for the Kingdom of God and His righteousness, and all these things will be given to you as well.

So do not worry about tomorrow, for tomorrow will bring worries of its own. Today's trouble is enough for today. (Matthew 6:25–34)

What a fantastic teaching! Jesus sounds like a Jewish Lao Tzu, and indeed the message of this sermon would ring true in the ears of any Taoist. Is Jesus saying we should simply sit back and let God provide for us? No. Jesus is saying that we should deal with today's troubles today, and leave tomorrow's worry for tomorrow. He is saying, Attend to the present, for the present is all you have. Worrying about the world to come, life after death, past or future reincarnations, heaven and hell, and all the other theological fantasies we invent to distract us from the present moment is of absolutely no value whatsoever.

WORRY OR GRACE—THE CHOICE IS YOURS

All that matters is this moment and how you engage it. There are two ways to engage this moment: with grace or with worry.

The opposite of grace is not God's enmity but your own anxiety. To think that God hates you is a kind of megalomania. It is like a wave on the ocean imagining that the ocean is doing to it what it is not doing to all the other waves. Nonsense. God "makes His sun rise on the evil and on the good, and sends rain on the righteous and on the unrighteous" (Matthew 5:45). God is *what* is happening. It is you who create a story as to *why* it is happening. And because your story revolves around you—what you do, what you say, what you think, what you feel—you spend most of your time worrying about how what you do, say, think, and feel will impact your future. This worrying does nothing to change the way you act, speak, think, or feel; it just gives you the illusion that doing so matters to God and therefore you matter to God.

Jesus is saying two things here. First that you do matter to God, but no more than anyone else matters to God. Second, that worrying about mattering to God is simply a waste of energy and time.

From the perspective of grace, worry is the great destroyer. Grace is the antidote to anxiety. When you are free from anxiety you are truly present to and in the moment. Without the distraction of worrying about what might be, you attend to what is.

In Theravada Buddhism this is called *sati,* mindfulness. In the *Satipatthana-sutta* the Buddha says:

> A *bhikkhu* (monk) applies full attention either in going forward or back; in looking straight on or looking away; in bending or in stretching; in wearing robes or carrying the bowl; in eating, drinking, chewing or savoring; in attending to the calls of nature; in walking, in standing; in sitting; in falling asleep, in waking; in speaking or keeping silence. In all these he applies full attention.[1]

Each action, each moment, has its own integrity. To be in harmony with it—to eat when hungry and sleep when tired, to paraphrase a Zen proverb—is to be in a state of grace. This is equivalent to King Solomon's notion that:

> There is a time for every matter under heaven: a time to be born, and a time to die; a time to plant, and a time to pluck up what is planted; a time to kill, and a time to heal; a time to break down, and a time to build up; a time to weep, and a time to laugh; a time to mourn, and a time to dance; a time to throw away stones, and a time to gather stones together. (Ecclesiastes 3:1–5)

Living gracefully is knowing what time it is, and acting in sync with it. If it is planting time, plant; if it is harvest time, harvest. But if your mind is on harvesting when it is time to plant, you will most likely plant poorly and harvest little if anything at all.

This is what the Hindu calls *karma yoga,* the way of detached action. "No one exists for even an instant without performing action; however unwilling, every being is forced to act by the qualities of nature," says the *Bhagavad-Gita* (3:5). Yet "always perform with detachment any action you must do; performing action with detachment, one achieves supreme good" (3:19). This is equivalent to the Taoist *wu wei,* noncoercive action.

Does this mean you should not plan for the future? No, it means that the future will not follow your plan. There is a plan for the future that arises out of the conditions of the present. If you wish to change tomorrow, you must engage today in a new way.

You don't self-consciously invent the new way, however. It is not the result of the scheming of narrow mind. Such scheming is only a recycling of old ideas and tiresome habits. About this Solomon says there is "nothing new under the sun" (Ecclesiastes 1:9). What is new must come from above the sun, beyond narrow mind.

Think of a ballerina. Her movements are highly choreo-graphed. She is not inventing the dance as she moves; she is being moved by the dance itself. If she is ungraceful, we can see the mismatch of dance and dancer. If she is filled with grace, the dancer and the dance are seamless.

Ask a skilled and graceful ballerina about her state of mind during a dance and she will speak to you of spacious mind. Her ego is lost to the dance. There is no dancer separate from the dance. The one who dances is the one who is danced. This is grace—the natural state of spacious mind.

NOTHING LEFT BEHIND

Why are we so rarely in a state of grace? Because we rarely have the courage to expend ourselves fully in the moment. We want to know that there will be manna tomorrow, and we imagine that the best way to know this is to hoard some away. This is narrow-mind reasoning: fearful, untrusting, lacking in faith.

The dancer holds nothing back. Each movement is full, complete, with nothing left over. This is living in grace. To live in grace you must use up each moment and become empty again. If you accept the fullness of each moment and engage it without hesitation and restraint, if you use it up and leave nothing in its wake, you will be empty again and ready for the next moment.

The problem is that narrow mind is not comfortable with grace. It doesn't trust God to provide. It is by nature a worrier and a hoarder. Narrow mind prefers to engage the world based on merit. According to this paradigm, there are winners and los-ers, leaders and followers, the successful and the unsuccessful.

God says, "I deal with each person according to merits, but to the person without merit I give grace" (*Deuteronomy Rabbah, Va-Etchanan*, 2:1).

The person of merit is the person trapped in narrow mind, preferring to operate on merit and seeing the world as a zero-sum game of winners and losers. The person without merit is the person at home in spacious mind, seeing each moment filled and full to capacity. There are no winners and losers in the world of spacious mind; there are only dancers at one with the Dance that is God.

THE PARADOX OF CULTIVATING GRACE

Cultivating grace is a bit of a paradox. You cannot get what you always and already have. There is nothing you can or need do to merit grace. All you need do is accept grace. The reason this is so difficult for us is that our hands are full. We are burdened by carrying the past and future around with us wherever we go, and have no room for the grace of the present moment. Cultivating grace means putting down the burden of time, and opening our hands to the timeless now.

There should be nothing left over at the end of your day, and nothing at the end of your life. You should have lived it all, for that is why it was given to you. If there is something left over, then you did not fully live while you were alive. You lacked grace.

This is not to say that you should fulfill every whim and desire that comes to narrow mind. That would be exhausting. The difference between fulfilling every whim and having nothing left over is that the former leaves you feeling wasted, the latter leaves you feeling blissful. When you live each day trusting in the manna, you end each day full, satisfied, and with nothing left over. You trust that tomorrow will bring its own fullness and there is no need to cling to what was. Living this way is living with grace.

How do we practice letting go and cultivating grace? By making Shabbos. We can drop all that we carry for one day each week and live as if we trust God's grace. In this way narrow mind learns the power of trust and grace. It stops worrying so much. It realizes that it can function more effectively without having to carry the past and future around on its shoulders. It begins to understand that it has a role to play in the present that has nothing to do with the role it imagines for itself based on past memory and future fantasy. Its role is to open to the wisdom of spacious mind and channel it into acts of lovingkindness in this and every moment.

Teaching this concept to teenagers in Miami, I would sometimes hold classes on the beach. I would give each student a plastic bucket and spoon and ask them to fill the bucket with seawater using the spoon. As they raced to fill their buckets they did not notice that I had sliced small holes in the bucket bottoms. Theoretically, if they raced back and forth quickly enough, they could keep a bit of water in the bucket, but if they stopped for even a moment the water would seep out the bottom.

It soon became obvious that the buckets could not be filled this way. "Alternatives?" I would ask, and watch happily as someone tossed his bucket into the sea and let it fill up of its own accord. "That is Shabbos," I would say. "Now how can we make it on land?"

Shabbos is surrendering to the greater reality of God as the place you are here and now. Making time for the Sabbath is an act of countercultural rebellion. You are saying "no" to the consumerist culture. You are saying "no" to the very idea that you have to earn a living, and "yes" to your own intrinsic self-worth. You might think this would be easy, yet the Sabbath had to be placed in the Ten Commandments to get people to pay attention to it. We are driven by the fear of scarcity and dare not trust reality to take care of us for even a single day. We live grace-less lives.

Shabbos is more than a day of rest; it is a day of grace. It is a day devoted to celebrating what is, rather than frantically trying to create what might be. It is a day for setting aside our addiction to the overwhelming flood of information from radio talk shows, twenty-four-hour cable news, and Internet feeds. It is a day for turning off the distractions of advertising that keep us hungry for things even as we stuff ourselves with them. It is a day without obligations: no gym, no errands, no homework, no housework, no driving kids from practice to game to mall to meals. It is a day for turning off the roar of external stimuli and allowing yourself to hear your Self, that still small voice of holiness so easily drowned out by what Wayne Muller, in his wonderful book *Sabbath: Remembering the Sacred Rhythm of Rest and Delight,* calls the clamor of "Buy me. Do me. Watch me. Try me. Drink me."[2]

I don't wish to see society return to a day of rest enforced by the laws of the state. Yet, it is sad to see how easily we have abandoned the Sabbath. I grew up in western Massachusetts during the days of Sunday Blue Laws. Most stores were forced to remain closed on Sundays. I don't remember any hardship as a result of this. As a Jew one might argue that forcing stores to close on Sunday made Saturday Sabbath observance more difficult, but, as I recall, the few kosher businesses in town were open on Sundays, and no one I know complained. At least not until neighboring Connecticut ended their Blue Laws and the Enfield Mall, less than a twenty-minute drive from my home, was open to Massachusetts consumers on Sunday.

Suddenly, everyone was going to Connecticut to shop on Sunday. What was odd was that we had never driven there before. The mall was open to us all week, and there was never a passion for shopping there. Only after the mall was open on Sunday did we discover the need for personal interstate commerce.

Of course, once neighboring Connecticut stores were pilfering Massachusetts shoppers, robbing local merchants of their sales and the state of its sales tax, Blue Laws in Massachusetts were doomed. Overnight, or so it seems to me in retrospect, Sunday became the day to go shopping. No one forced us to shop; no law was passed preventing us from resting on Sunday, but now that there was something "better" to do, and we ran off and did it.

A similar phenomenon is happening with Internet shopping. It used to be that stores closed by 9 or 10 p.m. But with the Internet you can shop 24/7. It is like living in a mall that never closes. The ability to buy whatever you want whenever you want makes all purchases impulse buys, and reduces the amount of thoughtful consideration that goes into shopping. While it is true that some people will use the Internet to investigate products and compare prices, for many more it is a window to a global kiosk that never closes.

I am not arguing against shopping, only noting how easy it is for us to give up rest. And not just rest, but all that goes with it: conversation, strolling, leisurely lovemaking, just "hanging out" with people. And, most of all, trusting that you can live without having to earn it.

This is the heart of Sabbath-consciousness and therefore grace: trusting that the universe is constructed to meet your needs if not your wants. *Want* is a wonderful word, and its dual meaning is very instructive. *Want* means both "desire" and "lack." When we want something, we are acknowledging a lack in ourselves or our lives. With the genius of advertising, however, these lacks are more imagined than real. We have a need for food, shelter, clothing, and companionship. We want fancy cuisine, huge homes, haute couture, and the perfect mate. There is no end to wants, and it is endless wanting, as the Buddhists remind us, that is at the heart of our dissatisfaction with life. While the Buddha doesn't use the word *grace* in this context, it seems to me that grace is the way of enlightenment.

The first of the Buddha's Four Noble Truths is that life as we live it is intrinsically unsatisfactory. The reason for this, the Second Noble Truth, is that we are forever craving. While it is easy to see how that craving translates into overconsumption and how overconsumption leads to personal debt and overwork, I believe the real craving is not for things but for permanence. We know that life is fleeting and we fear that we are but a momentary blip on the cosmic screen. This is so upsetting to narrow mind that it races around doing all it can to create the illusion of permanence. But deep down it knows that permanence is an illusion, and so behind all our doing is a haunting anxiety and fear.

The way out of this, the Third Noble Truth, is to put an end to craving, or, as I suggest, put an end to the need to live by the illusion of permanence. How? Here the Buddha offers us the Fourth Noble Truth of the Eightfold Path: Right Thinking, Right Speech, Right Livelihood, and so on. While I have no quarrel with the Buddha, I would like to add a ninth path: making Shabbos.

The Sabbath is the end of craving. The Sabbath is tossing the bucket of narrow mind into the sea of spacious mind and allowing your original divine nature to put an end to fear, anxiety, and craving.

LIVING GRACE THROUGH SABBATH KEEPING

Grace is living with radical trust, and the Sabbath is a day devoted to doing just that. For observant Jews, of course, there is a huge body of law and lore regarding the Sabbath, but for most of us, Jew and Gentile alike, the legal aspects of Sabbath observance are beside the point. In fact, they may even obscure the point. So let me suggest ways for making Shabbos that draw on Jewish tradition without necessarily imitating it.

Open and close your Sabbath with the lighting of candles. Even if the only Sabbath you can muster at this point in your life is just a few hours long, begin with the lighting of candles. Jewish tradition sets a minimum but no maximum to the number of candles you can light. The minimum is two—symbolizing the state of duality that usually precedes Shabbos. You come to the Sabbath with a split mind, maybe even a fractured heart. The week has been grueling, and you feel alienated from others and perhaps even from yourself. So you light multiple candles to honor where you are. Yet notice that the candles offer singular light. So you are beginning with two and aiming at one.

Offer a blessing. Begin your Sabbath with something like this: "May this Sabbath be a time for deepest surrender that I might discover the grace of God's living in me and as me." Adjust the pronouns if you are making Shabbos with family and friends.

Prepare a simple meal and offer thanks before eating it. For guidance in reciting a prayer before meals, look to Psalm 22:27: "The humble ate and were satisfied." Say something like, "Let this Sabbath meal be for us a time of humbling, of returning to our simple selves as the image and likeness of God. And, eating this way, may we be satisfied."

Bless children, loved ones, and friends. If you are sharing your Sabbath meal, make time for people to bless one another. If you are alone on Shabbos, offer blessings to those you love who are not present. You can use a variation on the *metta* prayer for this: "May you be blessed with simplicity; may you be blessed with humility; may you be blessed with grace."

Take a walk. Make time during your Shabbos to walk outdoors. "Walk like a camel," as Henry David Thoreau says in his time-less classic *Walking*. Thoreau says a camel thinks as it walks, so let your mind wander along with your body. Become what Thoreau calls a saunterer from the French *Sainte-Terrer,* a Holy Land pilgrim who wanders *sans terre,* without a specific home, for she is at home wherever her feet touch the ground.

Go slow. There is no rushing on Shabbos. You can't be late and there is no early. Do whatever you do with attention and care, and you will find a rhythm that is your Shabbos speed.

Pamper yourself. Take a long bath. Take a long nap. Surround yourself with fragrances you love, and books you want to read, and people with whom you really want to converse. Make love and give pleasure.

Make a to-do list for Shabbos. Put only one word on it: "Nothing."

Get off the grid. Don't bother with e-mail, web surfing, TV, or radio. Listen to music that soothes you. Or better yet, learn to play some yourself.

Close your Shabbos with candles. Judaism has a ceremony for closing Shabbos called *Havdallah,* meaning distinction. It marks the return to the week. What I love most about *Havdallah* and what I suggest you try is closing the Sabbath with a different kind of candle. A *Havdallah* candle is a single braided candle composed of wicks. While you began the Sabbath with two candles, honoring diversity even as you move toward unity, you end the Sabbath with a single candle that speaks of unity blossoming into diversity. The *Havdallah* candle reminds you not to mistake unity for uniformity and to open yourself to the complexity of the coming week without complicating it by wishing it were other than it is.

HAVDALLAH PRAYER FOR THE WEEK

Light your candle and offer the following prayer for the week:

> May this be a week of faith:
> Faith in truth, faith in love, faith in friendship, and faith in
>   You who manifests all things and their opposite.
> May my labors hasten the perfection of the world, and may
>   kindness awaken those deadened by despair.
> May this week arrive with gentleness, good fortune, blessing,
>   success, good health, prosperity, justice and peace.

May it be a week for uplifting the children and honoring the
aged.
May this be a week of constructive purpose for me, for my
loved ones, and for all who dwell upon this good earth.
Amen.

If you have the time and inclination, you might use a longer
blessing:

Blessed is the Source of Bliss who offers me a path to bliss.
May this be a week for setting aside expectations and surrendering to the simple truth of what is, that I may find
my way to what may be.

Blessed is the Source of Wisdom who offers me a
path to wisdom. May this be a week for heeding the intuitive voice that whispers within. May I be open to what
comes my way, trusting in Life and the One who manifests it.

Blessed is the Source of Understanding who offers
me a path to understanding. May this be a week for
cooling my desires and seeing things more objectively.
May I seek first to understand and only then to be
understood.

Blessed is the Source of Restraint who offers me a
path to restraint. May this be a week for holding back and
making room. May I uplift others and find in their success a bit of my own.

Blessed is the Source of Grace who offers me a path
to grace. May this be a week for reaching out to help and
reaching out to be helped, for offering love and opening
to it when it is offered.

Blessed is the Source of Balance who offers me a
path to balance. May this be a week of self-correction, listening to my needs and fulfilling them.

Blessed is the Source of Receptivity who offers me a path to receptivity. May this be a week for patience. May I resist the desire to change what is that I might first come to know what is.

Blessed is the Source of Victory who offers me a path to victory. May this be a week for overcoming obstacles, remembering that some walls need not be toppled, only walked around.

Blessed is the Source of Transformation who offers me a path to transformation. May this be a week for doing things differently. May I seek out new ways of encouraging mutual fulfillment, joy, purpose, and growth.

Blessed is the Source of Grounding who offers me a path to grounding. May this be a week for slowing down and settling in. May I attend to what needs doing and do it with fullness of body, mind, heart, and soul.

Living with grace is being true to the choreography of each moment, and knowing that the next moment has its own truth and may be completely different from this one. Cultivating a Sabbath-mind allows you to do just that.

EQUANIMITY IN THE MOMENT

Making Room in Your Heart for Reality

Equanimity purifies lovingkindness.
—*Theravadan Buddhist* Treatise on the Paramis

I picked up a copy of *USA Today* at a local convenience store and walked over to the checkout line. There was one person in front of me buying a variety of breakfast bars and a cup of coffee. As she rang up the items, the clerk said to the man, "How ya doin'?" To which he replied, "Can't complain." Neither one of them looked at each other as they spoke, and the entire exchange was of no real consequence to either of them, or to me. Of no consequence, that is, until the clerk looked over the man's shoulder and said to me, "How 'bout you? Can you complain?"

"Always," I said. And I meant it. I can always find things to complain about. The man in front of me nodded to me as he passed by and I noticed that he was wearing a baseball cap that said, "Jesus Loves You, But I'm Here to Kick Ass." I wanted to comment on the slogan but was afraid that I might provoke some serious kicking of my ass, so I restrained myself. I returned my attention to the cashier in time to hear her say, "I was readin' to my kid last night the story of what'shername and the three bears?" She ended her sentences as if they were questions.

"So you know the story? Goldilocks—right, that's her name—Goldilocks tries out the grits and beds and chairs and such? One is always too hot or too cold, or too hard or too soft, or too big or too small, and one is always just right. So I was readin' this story, and you know what? I realized that never in my entire life have I ever found anything that was just right. Can you imagine?"

Actually I can. I am rarely satisfied. Having said that, of course, I realize that I have just shattered any hope of your seeing me as a wise and spiritually profound teacher. But there it is.

Nothing is ever perfect. It is just what it is. Of course, some of my New Age friends say that everything being just what it is, is therefore perfect. I understand what they mean, but I find saying it pedantic and very annoying. Saying that reality is perfect just as it is, is a meaningless statement. Reality is reality is the most you can say. No need to label it perfect, imperfect, or anything else. It just is. Realizing this is at the heart of what it is to cultivate equanimity, the Sixth Attribute of Lovingkindness.

One of the traditional signs of the messiah in Judaism is equanimity; he endures without complaint. Indeed, I have heard several rabbis argue against Jesus as the messiah solely on the grounds that he complained in Matthew 15:34, saying, "My God, My God, why have you forsaken me?" (Jesus is quoting Psalm 22:2.) I'm sure they could come up with additional reasons if they had to, and I have never met a Christian who took this statement of Jesus as complaining. Even if Jesus did have a moment of doubt on the cross, so what? He was no less human than divine, and I imagine that I would have lots to say while being crucified that would be far less printable, let alone edifying.

When I think of equanimity I think of Mary, Jesus' mother, and the Buddha, his spiritual brother. I love to walk through museums that have art from Christian and Buddhist cultures.

The portraits of Mary that I have seen speak powerfully of equanimity.

Equanimity is the capacity to embrace what is as it is without getting bowled over by it. Chogyam Trungpa calls this forbearance:

> Whatever happens, you don't react to it. The obstacle to patience is aggression. Patience does not mean biding your time and trying to slow down. Impatience arises when you become too sensitive and you don't have any way to deal with your environment, your atmosphere. You feel very touchy, very sensitive. So the *paramita* [virtue] of patience is often described as a suit of armor. Patience has a sense of dignity and forbearance. You are not so easily disturbed by the world's aggression.[1]

Mary steals several scenes in Mel Gibson's *Passion of the Christ* because of her forbearance. Without ever saying a word, her face reveals a deep love for her son and great anguish over his suffering, and yet her expression seems to exist in a larger sea of calm that is healing even in its grief. When I watch her in the film or see her in the museum portrait gallery, I feel that sea of calm. She knows something that the agonized face of Jesus may not know: Even this suffering is all right. It too is reality.

I find the same wisdom when I stand before statues of the Buddha. I almost always bow to these sculptures, asking in this way to be blessed with the capacity to realize my own Buddha nature and thus manifest that sea of calm that he shares with Mother Mary. For a moment before both the Buddha and the Mother, I sense that I am that as well, but the moment always passes, and I take up my cross and move on.

The Hebrew for equanimity is *erech apayyim,* literally, long-faced. When you sit in silent meditation or prayer, notice what happens to your face. There is a softening around the eyes and jaw. There is an actual lengthening of the face that comes with the calm of this practice. In meditation, emotions still rise and fall, thoughts still come and go; you may sit with anger or grief, joy or hope, and yet your face is the same.

Compare the face of Mary when she is holding the baby Jesus to her face when she is holding the crucified Jesus. Can you see the same great calm in both? I do. There is a long-faced equanimity in both. Not that she is unmoved by either her newborn baby or her newly murdered son, but she is rooted in something larger than birth and death, and this something larger allows her to be true to the moment without being trapped in the moment.

The same is true of the Buddha's face. Sometimes I sit before a large statue of the Buddha and just stare back at him. I imagine him thinking, "I wonder what time it is? Have I been sitting here long enough? Is it time to go begging for lunch?" Once in the basement of a wonderful art museum in Cleveland, I watched with a mix of shock and humor as a tourist placed a can of V-8 juice in the Buddha's palm while bending over to tie his sneaker. It was done thoughtlessly, not maliciously, and it created a wonderful image. I suddenly knew the answer to the Zen koan, "What is the sound of one hand clapping?" as I imagined this stone Buddha suddenly coming to life, slapping his forehead with his free hand and saying, "Of course! I could have had a V-8!"

I don't think the Buddha would object to helping the man with his sneaker. I don't think the Buddha would be insulted or angered by what some might call an act of sacrilege. I think the Buddha would have done in real life just what his image did in the museum, held the man's drink until he was finished tying his laces, and then moved on.

That, to me, is the key to equanimity: engaging the moment and moving on. It is not about suffering in silence, but about accepting reality as it is each moment. And without such acceptance, engaging that moment with lovingkindness is impossible.

When you feel lovingkindness for others, or even yourself, is it because of who they are or because of who they might become? I asked this of a class I was teaching at a high school in Nashville and over half the class gave the latter answer. As one seventeen-year-old girl, speaking for the majority of her classmates, said, "I look beyond who a person is at the moment and see who they can become. And it is that potential person that I feel kindness toward."

I disagree. If you look to who a person can be, you are most likely projecting who you would like the person to be. You feel kindness toward your imagined person, and only tolerate the real person to the extent that she or he approximates your personal ideal.

Real lovingkindness is directed toward the person as she is: the image of God often distorted by the fearful furies of narrow mind. If you focus on the fury of narrow mind, you will get trapped in the chaos of the moment. But if you can allow the chaos to be chaotic, and open to that along with the deep, calm, and loving image of God that the other also is, then you will find equanimity and with it the capacity to engage the other with lovingkindness.

Equanimity has everything to do with expansiveness: how much room you can make in your body, heart, mind, and life for reality as it is in this moment. The story of Job again has relevance here.

I referred to Job earlier, but now let's take a closer look. Job was a righteous man caught up in the drama of uncertainty plaguing an all-too-human god. The story opens with Satan, Heaven's prosecuting attorney, returning to Heaven from a fact-finding mission on earth. Satan (which means "adversary" in Hebrew) reports to God, who asks Satan if he has seen Job. God extols Job's virtues and takes great pride in Job's love of God.

Satan, sensing a weakness in God, which is God's need to be loved, suggests that Job's love for God is contingent on God's largess toward Job. Job is wealthy, healthy, and the father of a large family. If he were deprived of these blessings, Satan argues, Job's love for God would sour. God takes the bait, and turns Job over to Satan for testing.

Always eager to reveal the underbelly of gods and humans, Satan kills off Job's children, destroys him financially, and plagues him with boils until Job is reduced to sitting amid the ruins of his life scratching his oozing sores. His life is so miserable that his wife urges him to curse God and die. Job refuses: "Shall we not accept the good and the bad from God?" (Job 2:10).

Let's pause here for a moment. Is Job displaying patience or equanimity? I would say the latter. If it were patience, Job would have answered his wife by saying, "It is not for us to judge what God does, let us wait and see what is to come." Yet Job does judge: There is good and there is bad. But knowing this he does not ascribe the one to God and the other to another. Job knows that God, to be God, must embrace and transcend all opposites. God must be, as God says in Isaiah, the creator of light and dark, good and evil (Isaiah 45:7). If God is only the source of good, then there must be a source of evil that is God's equal and opposite. A god limited to light, goodness, and justice is not the God of Job. Job's God—my God—is the Infinite that manifests all finite reality, the One Who transcends all ideas about God, no matter how ancient or sacred.

Hearing of his plight, Job's friends come to comfort him. In fact, however, they come to comfort themselves by making sense out of Job's suffering. If a righteous man can suffer, then God is capricious or morally bankrupt. Neither proposition supports their belief in a just God who rewards the good and punishes the wicked. So, rather than comfort Job, they try to get him to admit that his righteousness is a façade, and that he is at last getting his just reward.

I have heard Orthodox rabbis blame the Jews for the Holocaust, claiming that if the Jews of Europe had not aban-

doned God, God would not have abandoned them. I have heard
fundamentalist Christian ministers blame Americans for the
horror of 9/11: If we had only been tougher on gays and lesbians,
God would have kept the terrorists at bay. I have heard Muslim
clerics blame the victims of the tsunami, claiming that the people's lack of righteousness invited the divine punishment of
Allah. I have heard spiritual teachers tell breast-cancer victims
that their unresolved anger brought the disease upon them.
There is no end to people who protect their god from the terror
of truth by blaming the victim for the ravages of reality.

Job will have none of this. He refuses to admit to crimes he
has not committed, and he refuses to condemn God. This is not
patience, but expansiveness. This is true equanimity: Job knows
that God is bigger than our theologies. Job is anything but
patient in the sense of quietly enduring his plight. He refutes the
position of his friends and boldly challenges God to appear
before him and explain Godself. This is not patience in the con-
ventional sense. This is Gandhi's *satyagraha*, speaking truth to
power. Job won't curse God or give in to anger, but neither will
he resign himself to injustice.

It is here that the story becomes one of the great spiritual
texts of all time. God acquiesces to Job and appears to him in a
whirlwind. God is angry with Job's friends for their lack of faith
and their willingness to turn on Job. But God's attention focuses
on Job himself.

Rather than explain his testing of Job, God engages Job in
what the Buddhists call dharma (teaching) combat. Playing the
role of a Rinzai Zen master, God peppers Job with a series of *koans*,
puzzles designed to break the hold of narrow mind on one's thinking, and allow the greater truth of spacious mind to reveal itself.

Where were you when I spread out the foundation of the earth?
(Job 38:4). This is the Jewish version of the famous Zen koan,
"What is your face before your parents were born?" The answer
lies not in logic, but in the realization that spacious mind

transcends time. Where were you when God fashioned earth and sky? You were there! How so? Because your true essence is God.

Jesus made the same point when he said, *Before Abraham was, I am* (John 8:58). Jesus is saying that while narrow mind is bound by birth and death, spacious mind is birthless and deathless, beyond time, at one with the timeless One.

This is what God wants Job and, through Job, you and me, to realize. At first we are content with our lot, imagining that goodness comes to those who deserve it. We are caught up in the quiet pride of success. But in time we realize that the things we rely on to bolster our understanding of God and justice are transient. The certainty that we took for granted fades as the things we treasure turn out to be impermanent and unreliable. We are set adrift on a sea of uncertainty. This is the beginning of spiritual awakening.

God steps in to push Job to the next level of spiritual maturity. Can Job see that the temporal self and its treasures are not the whole story? Can he see his divine face that has existed from before his parents were born? True spiritual equanimity is not the willingness of narrow mind to put up with the sorrows of the temporal world, but the ability to see through the temporal into the timeless.

There is a trap here, however, a trap that Job avoids. The trap is that we imagine the timeless to be other than the temporal. God is not setting up a duality of time and timelessness. Rather God points out that time rests in the greater reality of the timeless. The eternal manifests in time, as time. God does not want us to see God separate from the things of this world, but to see God as the things of this world.

This is what is meant by the teaching of the Buddhist Heart Sutra: *Form is emptiness, emptiness is form*. Form and emptiness are both manifestations of that which includes and transcends form and emptiness.

Lots of teachers quote the first half of this passage of the Heart Sutra—form is emptiness—to make the point that the world as we see it is an illusion of no real value. Once I heard a famous European mystic say to a woman who had just been diagnosed with an inoperable cancer, "My dear woman, there is no you, there is no cancer, there is no problem!"

Sure: Form is emptiness. All I am and care about is a mix of chemicals, which are themselves just a bonding of molecules, which are themselves just dancing atoms, which are themselves mostly empty space. But tell that to my son, who counts on me to be there for him when he needs me; or to my banker who expects me to make my credit card payments on time; or to the driver in front of me stopped at a red light confident that I will not allow the emptiness of my red Saturn coupe to share the empty space of his yellow Chevy S-10 pickup truck. Emptiness is also form.

This is the message of the book of Job: God, reality, Tao, isn't one thing or another; it is everything and nothing at the same time. If you only understand that form is emptiness you can't enjoy life, and you have no compassion for the living. If you also know that emptiness is form, that form matters (pun intended), then you can take great joy in life no matter how the living manifest themselves to you.

Religion and spirituality often denigrate the temporal and urge us to take refuge in the timeless. This dualism is a trap in that it denies the holiness of the transient. God is creation, and to love God is to lovingly engage creation. Acting with lovingkindness in the world and toward the world reminds us that all things are a part of God.

Job sees through this dualism, saying, "In my flesh I see God" (Job 19:26). This is the same as Jesus holding up a piece of matzoh, saying, "This is my body," or the eighteenth-century Hasidic Kobriner rebbe holding up a slice of black bread before his Hasidim and saying, "You want to see God? Here, here is

God!" God is not other than the world, just greater than the world. And knowing this brings you the gift of equanimity.

Job never answers the questions God poses. Indeed, there is no answer other than awakening. Job exclaims that he now sees the timeless One in the temporal many and then chooses silence as the only rational response. And indeed it is.

The Hasidim tell a story that may help us here:

> A king once built a glorious palace and invited his people to come and see him. By means of mirrors he made it seem as if the palace were a maze of confusing corridors, preventing the people from finding him. He left sacks of gold and silver scattered around the entrance hall, and most who came took what they found and abandoned the quest to see the king. Seeing that no one was coming to him, the king called out to the people, saying, "These mazes are illusory. Push forward bravely and you will find me."

The equanimity we need is the equanimity to push forward bravely, testing the illusions of time, and finding the timeless that is the greater truth. How? Follow the model of Job. First, do not imagine that what befalls you, for good or for ill, has anything to do with you at all. You do not get what you deserve. You simply get what you get. This is *not* picking up the treasures strewn around the entrance halls.

Second, do not get trapped in a story about why what happens happens. Do not try to make sense out of life. Just live it as best you can. When friends share their theories, know they are sharing stories that support their presuppositions. Demand to see the truth for yourself without theory or story, the illusion of mazes and obstacles.

Third, see God in your own flesh. Ask yourself throughout the day, Who is it that is experiencing this moment? Who is it that is happy at this moment, or sad, or angry, or joyous, or worried, or calm? Who is it that is thinking, walking, typing, reading, talking, and the rest?

CULTIVATING EQUANIMITY THROUGH SELF-INQUIRY

Asking *Who is this?* is the equivalent of God questioning Job. As you ask, you realize that the asker is greater than the one being asked about, and yet both are you. The asker is spacious mind, pure awareness (Sanskrit *aham*) that holds and yet transcends the waves of time and space. This is finding the king, and finding the king is the birth of lovingkindness.

The master of this process is the great Indian sage Ramana Maharshi (1879–1950), who called it Self-Inquiry. As Ramana taught, you have thoughts, but you are not those thoughts; you have feelings, but you are not those feelings; you have desires, but you are not those desires. How do you know? Ask yourself: Who is it that is registering thought, feeling, and desire? As soon as the question is asked, there is a shift from narrow mind—the mind that identifies with thought, feeling, and desire—to spacious mind, what Ramana calls the Witness or Self.

The method, if it can be called that, is deceptively simple. By simply inquiring into experience, you see that there is a "you" that stands "outside" that experience. Of course, if you make that "you" into an object, it too becomes just another experience to be witnessed. This is the secret of true equanimity: It isn't another thought or feeling, it is simply the realization of spaciousness and the freedom that comes with it.

Language is not much help when exploring this, for language needs to objectify what it talks about in order to talk about it. This is why Job, along with all great mystics, ultimately takes refuge in silence.

Yet silence, too, can be reified and turned into an idol, so Ramana uses words to point beyond themselves. Perhaps the most famous way he does this is with his three-line teaching from the eighth-century South Indian Hindu saint Shankara: *The world is illusory; Brahman alone is real; Brahman is the world.*

The world is illusory. The world as narrow mind imagines it—a world of separate and competing objects; a world obsessed with the idea that certain thoughts and feelings can be held while others can be avoided; a world where you are your thoughts, feelings, and desires—is unreal, in the sense of being impermanent and temporary. The world of narrow mind is like a world conjured by a great novel or a gripping film. As long as you are willing to suspend the disbelief that reminds you that it is a fictional world, you can enter into that world and become wonderfully lost in it. Yet, when you realize that this is a fictional world, you naturally and effortlessly become aware of the "real" world. Ramana is saying that the so-called real world you return to after reading a good novel or watching a compelling film is simply another, albeit more compelling, fiction—this one of your own creation.

Yet, just as you can shift from the fiction on the screen or in the book to the fiction of narrow mind, so you can shift from the fiction of narrow mind to the truth of spacious mind. You only have to remember that it is there.

Brahman alone is real. Brahman is Ultimate Reality, God, Allah, Emptiness, *Tathata* (Suchness), Tao, and so on. Brahman is spacious mind, pure awareness. It is what the ancient Rabbis called *HaMakom,* the Place in which the world happens. Given the nature and limitation of language, as soon as we speak of Brahman, we cannot help but imagine that Brahman is a thing residing somewhere. This idea of Brahman is no less illusory than any thought of which you might become aware. You cannot imagine Brahman because you are not other than Brahman.

Brahman is the world. This teaching is critical. It is equivalent to the Heart Sutra's *Emptiness is form.* Yes, the world is illusory but that does not make it meaningless; it is also Brahman; it is also the Real. This is why Job never despaired. This is why great mystics do not succumb to nihilism. Yes, the world is a fiction, so enjoy it as you would a great film or novel.

One of my teachers told this story: The Greek philosopher Heraclites was walking beside a cool river on a hot afternoon. He noticed one of his students sitting on the bank staring at the water in which his friends cooled themselves. "Why don't you join them?" Heraclites asked. "Master, did you not say that one cannot step into the same stream twice? I cannot seem to find a way in." Heraclites said, "Yes, it is true that you cannot step into the same stream twice. The stream flows on and the place of that one step is long gone before a second can be taken." "Then how, Master, can I enter the stream at all?" "Like this," Heraclites said, and pushed the boy off his perch and into the water.

Just because a novel ends, just because a movie comes to a close, doesn't mean you cannot enjoy the story for what it is as long as it is. The story is part of the Real, just not all of the real. And while no part is permanent, every part is valuable. Knowing this is the key to equanimity.

Job is willing to sit in his story and let it play out. He does not ask God to change anything, only to explain it. Job does not ask that things be other than they are. He simply wishes to understand why they are the way they are.

So-called spiritual people often talk about their spiritual journeys, and the hardships of cultivating this or that state of mind. If *Brahman is the world,* however, there is nowhere to go and nothing to cultivate. You are already Brahman. Spacious mind is not something you lack; it is the ground in which narrow mind operates. Just look for yourself and see the truth of this. Who is it that is reading these words right now? Just inquire. And who is inquiring? Do you sense the spaciousness behind the narrow you? And who is sensing that?

There is no answer to Self-Inquiry. That is to say, you cannot point to spacious mind and say, "There it is! That is the real me!" The result of Self-Inquiry is always silence. There is nothing to say, no one to point, and nothing to point to.

When you engage the world from this place of silent equanimity, you engage it from the perspective of spacious mind. And when you engage the world from the perspective of spacious mind, you naturally engage it with lovingkindness. Without the need to defend narrow mind, without the fear and anger that often accompany narrow mind, you discover a world rooted in abundance rather than scarcity. You embrace this world courageously, lovingly, and with a desire to give of yourself and your possessions.

ACTS OF KINDNESS AND GIVING

Doing Right by Others

Rabbi Yochanan ben Zakkai and Rabbi Yehoshua were on their way out of Jerusalem. Seeing the destroyed Temple, Rabbi Yehoshua exclaimed, "How awful for us—the place where the sins of Israel could be forgiven lies in ruins." Rabbi Yochanan replied, "My son, do not grieve. We have another, equally effective form of atonement. What is it? Acts of kindness, for it is written: 'I desire kindness not sacrifice.'"
—Avot de Rabbi Natan

The relationship between kindness, the Seventh Attribute of Lovingkindness, and lovingkindness itself can be likened to that of a brushstroke and a painting. The first is a discrete action, the second the cumulative result of that and similar actions. When talking about kindness in the context of the Thirteen Attributes, the behaviors we will explore are measured in relation to what Jesus called "the least of these."

When the Son of Man comes in his glory, and all the angels with him, then he will sit on the throne of his glory. All the nations will be gathered before him, and he will separate people one from another as a shepherd separates the sheep from the goats, and he will put the sheep at his right hand and the goats at the left.

Then the king will say to those at this right hand, "Come, you that are blessed by my Father, inherit the kingdom prepared for you from the foundation of the world; for I was hungry, and you gave me food, I was thirsty and you gave me something to drink, I was a stranger and you welcomed me, I was naked and you gave me clothing, I was sick and you took care of me, I was in prison and you visited me."

Then the righteous will answer him, "Lord, when was it that we saw you hungry and gave you food, or thirsty and gave you something to drink? And when was it that we saw you a stranger and welcomed you, or naked and gave you clothing? And when was it that we saw you sick or in prison and visited you?"

And the king will answer then, "Truly I tell you, just as you did it to one of the least of these who are members of my family, you did it to me."

Then he will say to those at his left hand, "You that are accursed, depart from me into the eternal fire prepared for the devil and his angels; for I was hungry and you gave me no food, I was thirsty and you gave me nothing to drink, I was a stranger and you did not welcome me, I was naked and you did not give me clothing, I was sick and in prison and you did not visit me."

Then they will also answer, "Lord, when was it that we saw you hungry or thirsty, or a stranger or naked or sick or in prison, and did not take care of you?"

And he will answer them, "Truly I will tell you, just
as you did not do it to one of the least of these, you did not
do it to me."

And these will go away into eternal punishment, but
the righteous into eternal life. (Matthew 25:31–46)

This is the real meaning, message, and promise of kindness:
doing right by the powerless, the disenfranchised, those who can
be of no use to you and your quest for success. It is easy to be kind
to people who can be of help to you in achieving your dreams,
and doing so need not be a sign of anything but self-interest.
Jesus challenges you to measure your ability to actualize kindness in relation to those who cannot further your goals. On a
similar note, the Rabbis of Jesus' time said that one of the highest acts of kindness is to tend to the dead, for the dead are the
quintessential example of the least of these. While there are
many specific acts of kindness we could explore here, I will limit
myself to the four I find most compelling.

The first is making room for the suffering of others. While
acts of kindness are not predicated on another's suffering, the fact
is we are confronted by the suffering of others every day, and
unless and until we open our hearts to that suffering, our kindness
toward those who suffer will be more an act of avoidance than
love. To see the pain of another and to say "There but for the grace
of God go I" is to misread the situation entirely. The other's suffering is your suffering if you truly understand the nonduality of
self and other. The suffering of the least among us is yours as well,
and until you experience this directly you cannot act with true lovingkindness. Doing so is what the practice of *tonglen* is all about.

CULTIVATING KINDNESS THROUGH *TONGLEN*

While *tonglen* is a Tibetan Buddhist practice, I find a hint of
something similar in Psalm 104. Speaking to God, the Psalmist

writes, "You send forth your breath and renew the surface of the earth" (Psalm 104:30). This is exactly what *tonglen* does: uses the breath to transform the suffering of others. "We all carry within us our places of exile, our crimes, our ravages. Our task is not to unleash them on the world, it is to transform them in ourselves and others."[1] *Tonglen* is this art of transformation.

I do not claim to be an expert in *tonglen*. If you find this practice compelling, you should read *The Wisdom of No Escape* by Pema Chödrön, my first Tibetan Buddhist teacher. But for our purposes here, a taste of *tonglen* will suffice.

Begin by sitting quietly and opening up to the reality of the world as it unfolds within and around you. Invite the pain and suffering of the world to manifest itself to you. Imagine it as something dark, heavy, and hot. Breathe this pain into yourself as you would breathe in the aroma of a hot and spicy soup. Take in as much as you can, and allow it to find a home inside you. Now spin the black ball of suffering around and around and imagine that as it spins it becomes cooler, less dense, and clear. Watch as the dark ball of pain becomes white, light, and cool. Now breathe this transformed ball back into the world with the next out-breath. Breathe it out slowly, allowing it to dissipate in the air around you.

When you are able to do this comfortably, that is, when you are able to make room for the pain of the world in your own heart, move on to specifics. Imagine the dark ball as the pain and suffering plaguing loved ones or yourself. Simply be willing to take in that pain; do not resist it, but welcome it in without hesitation.

At first this may sound like a terrible practice, but I have not experienced it this way. Rather than weigh me down with the suffering of the world, *tonglen* reveals that spacious mind has room for infinite suffering. Just as the sky is never filled with clouds but is always greater than them, so spacious mind is never filled with suffering but holds it in a greater purity. Yet, holding the pain is not the way of *tonglen*. Spacious mind transforms the dark into the light and returns it to the world as a blessing. On a different theological plane, *tonglen* parallels the crucifixion of Jesus: It is a way to take upon oneself the pain of the world and transform it into love.

I find *tonglen* to be a powerful way to open myself to the pain of others. By breathing in that pain, I no longer find it alien. By making room for that pain, I make room for the one who is suffering from it. In this way I do not distance myself from the other and move beyond my fear of "catching" the pain by dealing with the person in pain.

I learned this from a hospice nurse I met when working with a young woman in my congregation who was dying of breast cancer. Although I visited her often, I could not shake the fear I felt upon doing so. Somehow I feared that if I got too close to this suffering, it would become my own. So I put a shell of professional distance between myself and her, one that made my visits totally ineffective.

The nurse, whose name I can no longer remember, took me aside one afternoon and said, "It is lovely that you visit so often, but you are still a stranger here. Of course we all know who you are, but you are not at home here, you are resisting the suffering that resides here. And in so doing you are resisting the love as well. You have to shatter the armor you wear in this house. You won't die. On the contrary, you might truly learn to live."

She then asked me if I was interested in learning how to shed the armor. When I said I was, she taught me *tonglen*. "This is how I live my day," she said, after teaching me the basics of the practice. "Whenever I encounter suffering I breathe it in. I have discovered that I can take in infinite suffering as long as I am willing to breathe out infinite peace. And the suffering does not stay. It is transformed and returned to the world as love. And so am I."

One complaint about *tonglen* that I have heard is that some who practice it become obsessed with suffering and no longer see the blessings of life. This has not been my experience. On the contrary, the more room I make for suffering the more room I seem to have for happiness.

This is so because happiness and suffering are opposite ends of a single spectrum. I cannot have the one without the other, and whenever I try to do so I find the experience is counterfeit. If I seek to avoid suffering by hiding in happiness, my happiness is reduced to a ploy, a tactic; I cannot surrender to it because it isn't genuine and I am always worried about suffering.

Author and radio commentator Dennis Prager, in his wonderful book *Happiness Is a Serious Problem,* argues that happiness is a moral issue. Happy people are more engaged, more generous, more likely to alleviate another's suffering. As simple, even simplistic, as it sounds, happy people are kinder people. Your happiness is good for everyone. But can you cultivate happiness directly? Can you simply make yourself happy?

I can't. Sometimes I feel happy and sometimes I don't, and trying to maintain a steady state of emotion is fruitless. Feelings are not directly controllable by the will, as my teacher David Reynolds and his philosophy of Constructive Living makes clear. If they were, I would feel happy all the time. I would not choose to suffer. But it isn't a matter of choice. Joy and sorrow, happiness and suffering go together. All we can do is be open to whatever comes.

Learning to be open is a side benefit of *tonglen* practice. What I discover as I breathe in suffering is that I am greater than suffering. Again, this is like the sky holding clouds while being greater than the clouds. I can hold the suffering and not be diminished by it. On the contrary, the more suffering I breathe in, the more space I seem to discover. So it isn't a matter of controlling anything, but rather of being open to everything.

Yet even if we cannot control the feeling of happiness, we can cultivate the conditions that are most conducive to it. For me that condition is gratitude. I have discovered that I am most happy when I am most aware of the gifts life bestows upon me moment to moment. I know of no better means of cultivating gratitude, and through gratitude happiness and kindness, than the practice of *Naikan*.

CULTIVATING KINDNESS THROUGH *NAIKAN*

I first learned *Naikan,* which is Japanese for "Inner Seeing," from Dr. David Reynolds, and have deepened my understanding of it through the teachings of the ToDo Institute, and its director, Gregg Krech.

Naikan is a contemporary and secular expression of Buddhist *bodhicitta* (kindness practice). The founder of *Naikan,* Yoshimoto Ishin (1916–1988), practiced *mishirabe:* going into a cave without food or water, and spending sleepless days and nights meditating on his life. Yoshimoto knew that *mishirabe* was powerfully transformative and healing but too austere for most people. He adapted the practice for ordinary men and women, at first using Buddhist temples instead of caves, and ultimately seeing secular *Naikan* centers flourish throughout Japan.

In the United States *Naikan* trainings are held at retreat centers, and usually last one week. Practitioners work alone, beginning the day at 5:30 a.m. and systematically reflecting on their life throughout the day. Every two hours or so the lone practitioner is joined by a *Naikan* facilitator for *mensetsu,* a face-to-face interview. The facilitator's role is to listen without comment to the recollections of the other.

You begin by reflecting on your relationship with your mother from birth to nine years of age. You ask three questions, and answer each in as much detail as possible: *What did my mother do for me? What did I do for her* (altruistically)? *What trouble did I cause her?* After working with memories of Mom, you move on to Dad, siblings, and others. There is no conversation with the facilitator. No help is offered or advice given. The facilitator does not respond to what you offer at all. You simply verbalize your answers to these three questions. The reflection and verbalization are themselves healing.

I am certain there is a formal explanation as to why and how *Naikan* works, but I don't know what it is. All I know is my experience with this practice. For me—and I am not unique in this, having spoken with many *Naikan* practitioners—the healing comes from the act of simply looking at what was and is, bolstered by the silence of the facilitator. The very fact that I get no response from the facilitator frees me to look at my reality with unclouded eyes. There is no payoff for being clever or wise or humble. I earn no points for being good and no demerits for being bad. I simply look into my past and report what I see.

In the practice of looking I slip into spacious mind; I become the sky rather than the clouds. I make room for what was and have no need to change it. And, as the practice continues, I have room for what is as well. *Naikan* is not about changing anything, but about seeing everything. And in the act of seeing there is a transformation that makes kindness not only possible but almost inevitable.

I will keep instructions in this practice to the bare bones so that you may practice it immediately, but, as with *tonglen,* I suggest you follow up any interest in *bodhicitta* and *Naikan* by reading Gregg Krech's *Naikan: Gratitude, Grace, and the Japanese Art of Self-Reflection,* and David Reynolds's *Handbook for Constructive Living.*

The general practice of *Naikan* as I use it regularly rests on asking three questions: *What have I received today? What have I given today? What troubles and difficulties have I caused today?* These questions can be asked in the open-ended manner written here, or personalized: What did my mother do for me today? What did I do for her? What troubles and difficulties did I cause her? You can do *Naikan* with anyone, though in both India and Tibet *bodhicitta* practice traditionally begins with your mother.

In the context of cultivating kindness, however, my focus is not on the distant past, but on the day just completed. I practice *Naikan* while lying in bed before falling asleep at night. I ask each question slowing, allowing plenty of time to review my day and receive my answer.

Asking the first question, *What have I received today?* I realize that I am being gifted by people all the time. Most of these gifts are quiet: Someone holds the elevator for me, someone picks up papers I dropped; but these gifts are gifts nonetheless, and realizing that I am receiving them begins to soften my heart. As Gregg Krech puts it,

> Often we take such things for granted. We hurry through our day giving little attention to all the "little" things we are receiving. But are these things really "little"? It only seems so because we are being supported and our attention is elsewhere. But when we run out of gas or lose our glasses, these little things grab our attention and suddenly we realize their true importance. As we list what we receive from another person we are grounded in the simple reality of how we have been supported and cared for. In many cases we may be surprised at the length or importance of such a list and a deeper sense of gratitude and appreciation may be naturally stimulated. Without a conscious shift of attention to the myriad ways in which the world supports us, we risk our attention being trapped by only problems and obstacles, leaving us to linger in suffering and self-pity.[2]

Asking the second *Naikan* question, *What have I given today?* is an act of brutal humility. I imagine that I am a generous person, doing acts of kindness for people without even thinking about it. But when I do think about it, when I spend some time actually listing those kindnesses, I discover that most of what I do for others is in fact self-serving. I give in order to receive. The list of answers to the second question is amazingly short. When I look honestly at my actions, I find that almost everything I do has some self-serving dimension to it.

This realization is humbling. Of course, you could say that all those gift-givers I encounter each day are also acting out of their own self-interest, but I don't really know that. All I know is, as Albert Einstein put it, "A hundred times a day I remind myself that my inner and outer life depends on the labors of other men, living and dead, and that I must exert myself in order to give in the measure as I have received and am still receiving." There is no judging of the motives of others in *Naikan;* there is only the honest recognition of your own. And when I do that, I find that I do very little.

Answering the third question, *What trouble, inconvenience, difficulty did I cause today?* often makes me laugh. I don't think of myself as a demanding person. I try to be helpful and supportive, and do not wish to be a burden to others. But when I make time to observe my behavior, I discover that I am making demands all the time, and the trouble and inconvenience I cause is immense. Not huge problems, mind you, but lots of little things. Whether it is in the classroom, at home, during my seminars—I make demands of people to meet my needs.

When seeking to cultivate kindness, I suggest the practice of *nichijo* or daily *Naikan*. Set aside twenty minutes before bedtime, and write down your answers to the three *Naikan* questions. Do not let yourself get caught up in the reasons why things happened; just note what happened. Be specific in your answers. If someone brought a cake to the office to share, write down what kind of cake. Take note of those little gifts you receive every day. Do not ignore things that people do because they "have to."

Tonglen and *Naikan* are inner-directed practices that will impact your behavior toward others. They complement each other. *Tonglen* makes room for suffering; *Naikan* makes room for gratitude. Together they transform how you experience the world. Now let's shift to outer-directed practices, and how you engage the world.

The practice that comes directly on the heels of *Naikan* is generosity: giving to others of our time, money, energy, and attention. The more you discover the giftedness of life, the more you wish to give back to others.

While there are many ways to gift other people (just look at your answers to *Naikan*'s first question), I want to focus on financial giving. I want to do this because my experience in the spiritual community is that people who call themselves spiritual are oftentimes loath to deal with money. They find it somehow evil and detrimental to their spiritual maturation. They misread the teaching, "The love of money is the root of all evil" (I Timothy 6:10), and imagine that money itself is the root of all evil.

Money is neutral. How you earn and spend your money is a moral issue. Buddhism, for example, insists upon Right Livelihood, earning money in a manner than does no harm. Judaism holds that products and produce that come from exploited workers is not kosher, or fit. But I want to focus on giving money away rather than earning it.

Whenever I speak about giving money away, someone always objects, "But what if I have no money to spare?" Yet when it comes to generosity, not having money to spare is the point. If I have extra cash, money I have no use for, and I give that money to you, I haven't been generous at all. I am simply giving you something I no longer care about. It is when I have to limit my own spending to help you financially that we can truly speak of generosity. If Bill and Melinda Gates donate five dollars to a charity, are they being generous? No. But when they donate millions, that indeed is generosity. When a beggar on the streets of Jerusalem takes a few coins from his pocket and gives it to other beggars (something that Judaism obligates Jewish beggars to do), that too is generosity. It is not the amount per se that matters, but the fact that giving financially impacts the giver in a significant manner.

Judaism and Islam are rich mines when it comes to generosity, and I want to share parallel practices from these traditions with you: *tzedakah* and *zakah*.

CULTIVATING KINDNESS THROUGH *TZEDAKAH* AND *ZAKAH*

The literal meaning of *zakah* is "purity," but it refers to the amount of money a devout Muslim is called on to donate to the poor each year. The link between these two uses of the term reveals its deepest significance. More than a form of charity, tax, or tithe, *zakah* is a spiritual discipline that purifies you from the delusion of ownership.

Everything you have is a gift from Allah, or rather it is on loan to you from Allah. Hence it is not yours to do with as you wish. A portion of what you receive must be purified from the concept of personal ownership. This is done by donating it to the poor. In Islam, failure to do so makes you a thief, holding on to something that does not belong to you. Doing so, however, also purifies the remaining monies for your use.

"While this is technically true," a Muslim friend of mine explained after I shared with him my understanding of *zakah*, "it misses the real power of *zakah*. *Zakah* does purify the goods, money, or property a person may have, but its real power is to purify the person himself. Selfishness and greed are the great temptations; they pollute the soul. *Zakah* purifies the heart from these traits. In one who receives *zakah*, there is no room for envy, greed, jealousy, and the like. Instead, such feelings are replaced with goodwill and gratitude. In the one who gives *zakah*, feelings of pride, superiority, egotism—all rooted in his material success—are replaced by feelings of compassion, lovingkindness, and humility. *Zakah* removes the distrust between the so-called haves and have-nots in society. While Islam supports private enterprise and is most compatible with capitalism, it does away with the excesses of capitalism by purifying greed and selfishness and replacing them with communal responsibility and kindness."

The practice of *zakah* is fairly straightforward, and while it is a practice incumbent upon Muslims, it is one that you may adapt to your own life as well. *Zakah* is an annual donation of 2.5 percent of your total worth after all bills and financial obligations are paid. *Zakah* is calculated at the end of the year, and the 2.5 percent rate is a minimum; you may give more if you choose. Total worth includes cash, stocks, land holdings, businesses, and the like. If you own immovable property, such as a building, you determine the rate of *zakah* based on the net worth of the income from the property and not the total value of the property itself. If, however, you earn money from building and selling houses or structures, then the rate is based on the total value of the entire property.

The Qur'an lists eight categories of *zakah* recipients: the poor who have no income; the needy whose income is insufficient to meet basic needs; new Muslim converts; Muslim prisoners of war who are being held for ransom and who can use the money to buy their freedom; Muslims who cannot meet their debt payments; *zakah* collectors (people hired to collect and distribute *zakah,* and who are paid out of the *zakah* that is collected); students who devote themselves full-time to the study of Islam; and Muslim wayfarers stranded in a foreign land and in need of help. While the restriction of *zakah* to Muslims may be incumbent upon fellow Muslims, non-Muslims who wish to practice *zakah* should not feel constrained.

The Jewish principle of *tzedakah,* from the Hebrew *tzedek,* "justice," is the forerunner of *zakah*. Often mistranslated as "charity," *tzedakah* is better understood as "fairness." Giving both *tzedakah* and *zakah* is not a matter of *caritas,* heart, from which the word "charity" comes, but of one's obligation to a financially fair and just society. Giving to the poor is an obligation binding even upon the poor themselves. In Islam everyone whose end-of-year net worth exceeds fifteen dollars is required to give *zakah*. In Judaism Jews are obligated to give at least 10 percent of their income to the poor. *Tzedakah* is not limited to Jews and is made available to all who are in need.

MAIMONIDES' EIGHT LEVELS OF *TZEDAKAH*

The medieval Jewish philosopher Maimonides lists eight levels of *tzedakah:*

1. Giving grudgingly
2. Giving less than you should, but doing so cheerfully
3. Giving after being asked
4. Giving before being asked
5. Giving when you do not know the recipient, but the recipient knows you
6. Giving when you know the recipient, but the recipient does not know you
7. Giving when both giver and receiver are unknown to one another
8. Enabling the recipient to become self-sufficient and no longer in need of *tzedakah*

While the laws of *tzedakah* and *zakah* for observant Jews and Muslims can be quite complicated, those of us looking for general guidelines will find the notion of giving between 2.5 and 10 percent of one's income or worth (your choice) to be sufficient. In addition to large giving at the end of the year, let me suggest three smaller disciplines from my own practice of *tzedakah*: a *tzedakah* purse, a *tzedakah* box, and a Free Loan Society.

A *tzedakah* purse is a small bag or wallet containing money that you intend to give to the poor you encounter on the street today. Many of us find it difficult to navigate the numerous poor and needy people on the sidewalks of our hometowns. We don't know if we should give and how much we should give. Some prefer to give through institutions and pass the beggar without dropping a single coin in her cup. Others will give over and over again until their pockets are empty. There is a middle way.

First determine how much money you are going to donate. Then decide how much is going to go to institutions and how much to individuals on the street. Send your check to the former, use your *tzedakah* purse for the latter. Each day put the amount of money you are to give to the poor that day in the purse. When asked for change, draw it from that purse. This money has already been designated for the poor, so any resistance on your part to giving it away should be, as the Muslims teach, purified. Just give it. When the purse is empty, your obligation for the day is done. You may choose to give more, but you are not obligated to do so. Using a *tzedakah* purse takes the guesswork and the ego out of giving.

A *tzedakah* box is a small container you keep at home into which you toss spare change when you come home. The money in that box is dedicated to a specific cause or organization. You can have one box for a local food bank, another for a homeless shelter, and another for a scholarship fund. When a box is full, count the contents and send a check for that amount to the designated recipient.

My third suggestion, a Free Loan Society, is a bit more complicated. Traditionally every Jewish community would establish a Free Loan Society where people could go for small, short-term, interest-free loans. When I was the rabbi of Temple Beth Or in Miami, our synagogue had such a society, offering loans of up to five hundred dollars to people in crisis.

A Free Loan Society is based on trust. The lender trusts that the borrower is honest, truly needs the money, and will repay the loan as soon as possible. Borrowers know that the loan fund depends on their honesty; if they fail to repay the loan, the society will not have the funds to help others in the future. In the twenty years I was rabbi of Beth Or, we did not have a single defaulted loan.

You can create your own Free Loan Society with family or friends. Each year members of the society are obligated to put an agreed-upon amount of money in the fund, and a rotating system is put in place to have someone responsible for dispersing the money. If the society is small enough, the members can decide together on how the money is dispersed, but if this falls on one or two people, their obligation is to report only amounts and not recipients. The latter are to remain as anonymous as possible.

While in no way intending to lessen the importance of giving *zakah* and *tzedakah*, there is another kind of currency that must be purified in the cultivation of lovingkindness, and that is speech.

CULTIVATING KINDNESS THROUGH HOLY SPEECH

The Baal Shem Tov, founder of the eighteenth-century Jewish mystical movement called Hasidism (from the Hebrew word *chesed*, meaning "kindness"), taught that each of us is born with a fixed number of words to speak, and when we have spoken the last of these we die. How would your everyday speech change if you really believed that?

I remind myself of this teaching all the time. Since I don't know how many words I was born to speak, and have no idea how many words I have left to speak, do I want to die for the words "You idiot!"?

The words we use can hurt as well as heal, and speaking kind words figures prominently in the sacred art of lovingkindness. Yet there is more to kind speech than saying nice things. An old Jewish folktale makes this quite clear:

> There was once a man who loved to gossip. He loved the attention it brought him, and could not stop himself from speaking about others, sometimes sharing the good they did, but most often sharing the mistakes they had made.

In time, however, he realized the harm his speech was causing and he sought to make amends. He went to his rabbi and explained the situation, and asked how he could make amends.

The rabbi thought for a moment and instructed the man to go the marketplace and purchase two of the finest feather pillows he could find. He should then take his pillows to the top of the mountain overlooking the village, tear them open, and spill the feathers into the wind.

The man was surprised and pleased at the rabbi's advice. He thought repentance would be much harder than this. So he ran to the marketplace, purchased his pillows, and within an hour had scattered their feathers to the wind.

He returned to the rabbi all aglow. He was ready to be forgiven for his gossiping. Not just yet, the rabbi told him. There was one more thing to do. He had to return to the mountain and repack the pillows with the feathers he had scattered.

"But that's impossible," the man said. "Those feathers have gone everywhere, there is no way I can take them back now."

The rabbi nodded solemnly and said, "What is true of feathers is true of words. Once spoken they can never be retrieved. The harm caused by gossip cannot be undone."

Gossip is something people love to do. Not that they will admit this, necessarily. On the contrary, most people think of themselves as being above this kind of talk. Don't you believe it. Gossip is among the most prevalent forms of communication we have.

Try an experiment. For the next twenty-four hours take note of how often you find yourself talking about other people and listening to friends and associates talk about other people.

Buy one of those inexpensive counting devices at a local hardware store to help you keep track. At the end of the twenty-four hours, check your tally. If you were vigilant, you will be surprised at just how often you were caught up in gossip.

Why? Because people are forever comparing themselves to others, sometimes building people up, sometimes tearing them down. It is our passion for comparing that leads us into gossip. When you compare yourself with others, someone always wins and someone always loses. That is why you are making the comparison in the first place. Not that you always win; sometimes you like to lose in order to feel humble, or victimized, or helpless.

Does this mean you can never talk about people? No. It means that you can never talk about people without being very careful about what you say and how you say it. For example: A friend of mine was recently honored with a humanitarian award. I was so proud and excited that I shared the news with a few friends who knew her. They, too, were enthusiastic and complimentary. But within just minutes of mentioning her award, someone remembered a time when our award-winning friend was less than helpful on a project another person was engaged in. In other words, we reminded ourselves, she may have won this award, but she is no saint.

Why did we have to carry the conversation on long enough to put our friend down a bit? Because in our rush to compare ourselves to her, we felt we were losing and had to even things out.

There was nothing wrong with my sharing another's good fortune. If I had been able to catch the conversation before it turned, and had moved on to another subject, we might have managed to avoid gossiping about our friend. But I hadn't been able. It had all happened so fast. That is why, when it comes to avoiding hurtful speech, the rule is to avoid talking about other people when they are not present.

But what about being honest with people? What if someone asks you about another person? Maybe a friend is thinking about dating a person you know, and she asks you your opinion of him. What if you know he lacks integrity when it comes to dating and tends to take advantage of women? Aren't you obligated to tell what you know?

Yes and no. First, you have to be sure that what you know is true. Second, you have to be clear in your mind as to why you are sharing the information. Is it to help your friend, or is it to make sure she isn't getting a date when you don't have one? Third, you have to speak the truth in a way that conveys what is true without the embellishment or added drama that can lead to unnecessary suffering. That is the way of lovingkindness.

Avoiding hurtful speech has as much to do with how you say something as it does with what you wish to say: Keep it simple; stick to what you know to be true; and move on.

Two thousand years ago the Rabbis asked this question: It is customary to compliment a bride on how beautiful she looks at her wedding, but what if this particular bride doesn't look beautiful at all? Is it permissible to lie? Is it better to avoid saying anything than to say something that isn't true?

The Rabbis debated this as a means of exploring some of the subtleties of hurtful speech. They concluded that lying isn't acceptable, but neither is hurting a person with the truth. And avoiding talking to the person sends a negative message all by itself. So what is a person who seeks to practice lovingkindness through speech to do?

Find a way of complimenting the bride without violating the truth or her feelings. For example, the Rabbis said, Say to her, "You never looked more radiant" or "You never looked lovelier" or "You are positively glowing tonight." You get the idea. Find a way of being for others—not down on them—whenever possible.

Yet there are times when being for others does mean sharing harsh truths. For example, if a friend is thinking about buying something and asks your opinion about the purchase, you are free to tell her what you think. But if your friend has already purchased the item and is committed to that purchase, you are like the rabbi at the wedding—say something supportive even if you are opposed to the purchase.

The point here is that in the first case the purchase was not made, and your opinion would help the person decide whether or not to make the purchase. In the second case, the purchase was made and final, and a negative remark from you, no matter how heartfelt, would do nothing more than hurt the person needlessly.

Given this, it is not gossip to warn a person about potential dangers resulting from a not-as-yet finalized business or personal relationship. Just be sure what you are about to say is true, and be careful to tell what you know without exaggeration. Do not pass on hearsay, and be clear about your intent in sharing this information: The only reason to do so is to help another and not to further your own ends.

There is a special kind of speech that needs to be mentioned here: telling people hurtful things that other people may have said about them. We excuse this by saying, "It is for his own good to know what is being said about him." But is this always so? Too often we share this kind of information just to put a person down without getting dirty ourselves. And we love the drama that results when we help person A discover the hurtful things person B has said about him. Be very aware of what you are doing and why you are doing it. In most cases you will find this to be a very harmful and debasing kind of talk.

When you are ready to tackle the issue of speech, there are nine guidelines that will prove useful to you. They are adapted from the eighteenth-century Jewish sage Rabbi Israel Meir Kagan, who is called the Chofetz Chaim (Seeker of Life).

CHOFETZ CHAIM'S GUIDELINES FOR RIGHT SPEECH

1. Do not spread a negative image of someone, even if that image is true.
2. Do not share information that can cause physical, financial, emotional, or spiritual harm.
3. Do not embarrass people, even in jest.
4. Do not pretend that writing or body language or innuendo is not "speech."
5. Do not speak against a community, race, ethnic group, gender, or age group.
6. Do not gossip, even to your spouse, relatives, or close friends.
7. Do not repeat gossip, even when it is generally known.
8. Do not tell people negative things said about them, for this can lead to needless conflict.
9. Do not listen to gossip. Give everyone the benefit of the doubt.

Another eighteenth-century rabbi, Israel Salanter, founder of *Musar,* the school of Judaism focused on virtue, taught that the key to righteous living is to "say what you mean, and do what you say." This is not as easy as it may sound. Saying what you mean requires you to be clear about what is happening, and to respond to it from spacious rather than narrow mind.

The first step to saying what you mean is getting some distance from what is happening. One way to get distance is to use the method of self-inquiry and ask, "Who is reacting this way?" Getting distance means shifting from narrow mind to spacious mind.

Once this shift is made, you can look at the truth of the situation without getting blown away by it. You can see more clearly the ramifications of what is happening and the implications of your various response options. You can sift through these and choose the one that is most likely to promote compassion, mercy, justice, and humility so that when you speak, your words will reflect the best that is in you.

As difficult as this may be, doing what you say can be even more challenging. Once you have committed yourself to something, unless that something violates the attributes of lovingkindness you are trying to cultivate, you must follow through. No excuses.

We often say the right thing, and then find ourselves resenting having to do the right thing. Talk is cheap, however; our behavior is what truly defines us. Listen carefully to your speech; say only what you mean, and do everything you say.

This requires you to slow down your normal pace of communication. So often we talk just to talk. We say things for the sake of saying things. We exaggerate to make what we say more interesting. We promise things before we have determined whether or not we can fulfill the promise.

Ask yourself three questions before you speak:

1. Is it true?
2. Is it kind?
3. Is it necessary?

There are things you can say that are true and cruel. Sometimes it is necessary to say them; more often it is not. No one can judge this for you, however. Simply focus on the quality of your speech and see that what you say is in line with the attributes you are trying to cultivate.

Sometimes, however, you will catch yourself saying things that are not really true. You will get caught up in a story you are telling and fall into the trap of gossip or self-aggrandizement.

Listen carefully to what you say as you are saying it, and be prepared to stop midsentence to correct any false or exaggerated statements you may be making. This may seem awkward at first. You have to admit to being less than honest and accurate; you will have to admit (if only to yourself) that you are pushing an agenda and not really speaking plainly and honestly. Yet the more you catch and correct yourself, the more plain and honest your speech will become, and the simpler your life will be.

Faulty speech is one of the primary ways we complicate our lives. Life is naturally complex. We make it needlessly complicated when we fail to engage the reality of the moment, and distort or deny what is true. We complicate things when we do not say what we mean and do not do what we say.

CHAPTER SEVEN

THE TRUTH OF OUR STORY

Embracing the Paradoxical Truth of Not-knowing

I search after truth, by which man never yet was harmed. But he is harmed who clings to his deception and ignorance.

— *Marcus Aurelius,* Meditations, vi. 21

One of the most memorable lines in modern cinema comes from Aaron Sorkin's 1992 film *A Few Good Men* starring Jack Nicholson as Colonel Nathan Jessep and Tom Cruise as Lieutenant Daniel Kaffee. During a heated courtroom exchange, Jessep says to Kaffee:

> JESSEP: You want answers?
> KAFFEE: I think I'm entitled to them.
> JESSEP: You want answers?
> KAFFEE: I want the truth!
> JESSEP (screaming): You can't handle the truth!

Colonel Jessep is right; we can't handle the truth. Why? Because the truth undermines the stories we tell ourselves, and we place more stock in the story than in the reality it masks.

[Jesus said to a paralyzed man,] "Son, your sins are forgiven." Now some of the scribes were sitting there, questioning in their hearts, "Why does this fellow speak in this
way? It is blasphemy! Who can forgive sins but God
alone?" At once Jesus perceived that they were discussing
those questions among themselves; and he said to them,
"Why do you raise such questions in your hearts? Which
is easier to say to the paralytic, 'Your sins are forgiven,' or
to say, 'Stand up and take your mat and walk'? But so
that you may know that the Son of Man has authority on
earth to forgive sins"—he said to the paralytic—"I say
unto you, stand up, take your mat and go to your home."
And he stood up, and immediately took the mat and went
out before all of them; so that they were all amazed and
glorified God, saying, "We have never seen anything like
this!" (Mark 2:5–12)

A close reading of this text reveals the link between truth and
lovingkindness. Jesus says, *Son, your sins are forgiven.* The scribe's
response to Jesus' words reflect the assumption made by the
author of this Gospel, namely that Jesus himself is forgiving the
man's sins. But does he? Jesus does not say, "Son, I forgive you
your sins." All Jesus does is state that the man's sins are already
forgiven. Jesus isn't the cause of forgiveness; he is the herald
of forgiveness. This is part of the Good News that Jesus
brings: God's forgiveness is absolute and timeless; you are
already forgiven.

How can this be? It is so because, as Judaism then and now
teaches, God's love is *ahavah rabbah,* infinite love. Infinite love is
unbounded, unconditional, present here, now, and always. God's
love, and therefore God's forgiveness, is constant.

Jesus then says to the scribes, *Which is easier to say to the paralytic, "Your sins are forgiven," or "Stand up and take your mat and
walk"?* We might say that forgiving sins is the more difficult, but

Jesus would disagree: "This fellow's paralysis is caused by the guilt he feels over the sins he has committed. If I were to order him to stand up and walk, he would not be able to do so because the cause of his paralysis is still in place. So I remove the cause by reminding him that God's love is greater than his sin, and God's forgiveness is greater than his guilt. Without the guilt to weigh him down, he can get up and walk. I did not remove the cause, I simply reminded the man that the cause is already removed, and it is only his telling himself otherwise that prevents him from walking."

What is true of this fellow in the Gospel is true of us as well. We are all weighed down by the guilt we feel over the sins we have committed. We are paralyzed by the story of our paralysis. We need a new story. And that is exactly what Jesus offers here. When you realize that God's love is greater than your guilt, your guilt fades and your paralysis ends. This, I think, is what the Buddhist teacher Jack Kornfield means when he writes, "The pains of our past cannot be released—until we touch them with healing and forgiveness."[1]

Jesus' compassion for the paralyzed is rooted in his capacity to see that our paralysis is rooted in our story. "Truly I tell you, unless you change and become like children, you will never enter the kingdom of heaven" (Matthew 18:3). Why? Because children are not yet locked into a story. Whatever guilt they feel is temporary, because they have not yet fallen into the habit of telling guilt-laden stories that create paralyzed and guilt-ridden selves. And at the heart of your story is the erroneous notion that guilt trumps God. The truth we cannot handle is the truth of God's unconditional love. This is the truth that "will make you free" (John 8:32); this is the truth that you need to grasp in order to cultivate lovingkindness. And it is as true for Jews, Buddhists, Hindus, and others as it is for Christians.

The problem is that you cannot grasp it directly. You are so locked into paralyzing stories that you cannot think otherwise.

This is our paralysis. So to cultivate truth we have to go at it from a different direction. Rather than affirm the truth of infinite love and the freedom it bestows, we have to see past the falsehood of the stories we already tell ourselves and allow them to drop away.

How do you know something is true? You look at it objectively. The problem is that the "you" that does the looking is conditioned by the very thing you are looking at, which makes objectivity impossible.

I am not talking about scientific truth, or the truths of mathematics. I am not referring to the simple facts of my physical existence, the kinds of facts that you can read on my driver's license, for example. I am talking about the deep psychological "truths" that define me as me. I am talking about my belief system. I cannot be objective about my most deeply held beliefs because I cannot make an object out of them. If I cannot be objective, I cannot know for certain if what I believe to be true is in fact true. The truth is that we don't know what the truth is. This is the beginning of wisdom.

You might raise an objection here: If lovingkindness depends on truth, and truth is fundamentally unknowable, then how is lovingkindness even possible? The answer is that the truth I am concerned with, the truth at the root of lovingkindness, is the truth of unknowability. Lovingkindness doesn't come from knowing what is what, but from knowing that you don't know what is what. Not-knowing rather than knowing is the key to lovingkindness. Not-knowing leads to genuine humility, and humility is the prerequisite for lovingkindness.

The Hebrew book of Genesis tells us that God created *adam* from *adamah*, the earthling from the earth. Adam was not originally a person's name, but the name of a species: humanity, from *humus*, earth. The word *humility* comes from the same Latin root. To be humble is to return to your original nature as the image and likeness of God; that is, God manifest as you in your time and place. In the first telling of this story (Genesis 1:24–30)

God creates *adam* male and female, and their task is to steward the rest of creation. In the second telling, the first *adam* is male only, and his mission is to till the earth (Genesis 2:5), and without this work the earth could not bring forth her bounty.

The two stories don't jibe. In the first story *adam* emerges after the earth has brought forth trees, herbs, plants, and so on. No human intervention was required. In the second it is because of human intervention that the earth reaches her potential for life. To reconcile the two stories the Rabbis invent further stories. Here is the one I like best:

> When we are told in the second story that the task of humanity is to "work the soil," the soil to which Torah is referring is not the earth in general, which is doing quite well without human help, but rather the soil that becomes humanity: God "formed the earthling from the dust of the earth, and blew into its nostrils the breath of life; and the earthling became a living being" (Genesis 2:7). The soil we are to till, then, is the soil of self.

To till the soil means to turn it over: to break up the hard and dry patches, to let in fresh air and light. Without this tilling the soil becomes lifeless. Torah is telling us to continually till the soil of self, to break up the hard, dry, and lifeless patches And what are these patches? The deeply held opinions we mistake for truth.

Israeli and Palestinian babies don't come into the world hating one another. They have to be taught to hate. Hindu and Muslim babies do not emerge from the womb angry with one another. They have to be taught this anger. Acts of anti-Semitism, racial discrimination, misogynistic behavior, homophobic actions, and genocide are impossible without fear-based opinions masquerading as objective truths.

Why is truth central to lovingkindness? Because lovingkindness is an action that requires clear seeing; and seeing clearly—that is, seeing without the filters of this or that system of belief—is what truth is. The issue is not which belief is true, but can you live without belief altogether?

Krishnamurti, one of the greatest philosophers of the twentieth century, argues that this is the only way we truly live at all. He calls the truth-filled mind, the mind free from beliefs and sacred opinions, the "religious mind." "You cannot be religious and yet be a Hindu, a Muslim, a Christian, a Buddhist. A religious mind does not seek at all, it cannot experiment with truth. Truth is not something dictated by your pleasure or pain, or by your conditioning as a Hindu or whatever religion you belong to. The religious mind is a state of mind in which there is no fear and therefore no belief whatsoever but only what is—what actually is."[2] How do we live with "religious mind," or what I call spacious mind? By letting go of our "truths," and I know of no better way to do this than through the work of Byron Katie.

QUESTIONING YOUR TRUTH

Sometime during the 1970s, Byron Katie, or Katie as she prefers to be called, a California wife, mother, and successful businesswoman in her thirties, became severely depressed. The depression deepened over a ten-year period, and she obsessed about suicide. Then, at one of her lowest moments and seemingly out of the blue, she had a life-changing realization.

Katie realized that her depression descended on her when she insisted that life conform to her beliefs, but when she allowed reality to be reality she was at peace. Rather than try to change the world to fit the belief, she suggests we question the belief and engage the world as it is. As Katie puts it, "If you try and fight reality you will lose ... but only 100 percent of the time." This realization ended her depression, and filled her with a sense of lovingkindness for all. Over time Katie developed a simple method for helping others question their beliefs. She calls her method The Work.

As it pertains to the cultivation of lovingkindness, The Work rests on asking four belief-busting questions. The four questions are designed to expose faulty beliefs about how reality should be. Once you recognize the false nature of these beliefs, the belief falls away, and you are free to "take up your mat and walk on."

Chances are you have experienced something like this many times in your life. To cite but one example, a friend of mine told me recently that he was deeply hurt by a caricature his son had drawn of him during a "crayon session" at kindergarten. "I am doing my best to lose weight," he told me, "and I often use the phrase 'green with envy' when talking about people who can eat whatever they want and not get fat. But my kid drew this grotesque cartoon of me all bloated and green. My wife put it up on the refrigerator. I think she thinks that if I see how my son sees me I won't go foraging for food. I'm hurt by him and pissed at her."

"Did you tell them how you feel?" I asked.

"No way. I don't want them to know they got to me."

"Are you sure you got the drawing right? You know for a fact the picture is you?"

"Of course it is me. Big, fat, green, purple suit ..."

"Purple suit?"

"Yeah, he colored in this messed-up purple suit on me and ..."

At this point I burst out laughing. My friend was not pleased.

"Listen," I said. "Go ask your son who he drew. It isn't you. I guarantee it. It's the Hulk. The Hulk, Bruce Banner, the comic book, the new movie?"

"You're kidding," he said. I wasn't kidding and I wasn't wrong. And as soon as my friend found out he was wrong, the truth set him free. Where did all his anger go? It just melted away with the ending of his false story. This is the power of truth.

Here are Byron Katie's four questions with a few follow-up thoughts of my own. Ask yourself these questions whenever your beliefs paralyze you.

Question 1: Is it true?

Think about this before you answer. If your answer is "no," go to Question 3. If your answer is "yes" go to Question 2.

Question 2: Can you absolutely know that it's true?

The key word here is *absolutely*. While you might argue that you are absolutely sure that 2 + 2 = 4, little else in your life commands such certainty. I am rarely troubled by the certainties of mathematics, but I am constantly being tripped by more psychologically charged beliefs such as "I should weigh less than I do"; "He shouldn't treat me the way he does"; and "She should love me more." Do I absolutely know these beliefs are true? No.

This may not be as easy as it sounds. We are very attached to our beliefs. We want things to be the way we imagine they should be. But our sense of how things *should* be is most often rooted in a belief that has no objective truth to it. It is true that I would *like* to weigh less than I do, but is it true that I *should*? Given my eating and exercise habits, I should weigh exactly what I do weigh. Reality is never other than what the conditions for reality allow. Things are exactly as they are supposed to be, given the conditions that exist. If you want to create a new reality, change the conditions that underlie the old one.

Question 3: How do you react when you think that thought or tell that story?

How does that belief impact you physically? Emotionally? Intellectually? Spiritually? How do you treat yourself when that story is playing out in your mind? How do you treat others during that time?

I can only answer this for myself, and I know for certain that when I operate based on my beliefs, I am never at my peak. Why? My beliefs are always at odds with reality, and this dissonance is inherently paralyzing. For example, I believe that my friends should forgive me when I hurt them. If they don't, I shift my focus from being forgiven to their inability to forgive, from dealing with reality to dealing with my belief. I am now free to ignore the pain I have caused and focus on the pain they are causing me. I get angry and my anger paralyzes me in my original quest for forgiveness. When I allow my beliefs to guide my actions I tend to put lovingkindness aside and focus on willful manipulation to get what I want. This makes me anything but loving and kind.

Question 4: Who would you be without that belief?

How would you live differently if you knew that a certain belief were untrue? I am not sure. My experience is that without my beliefs, there is no fixed "me" that I can point to as my authentic self. What I can say is that when I question my beliefs in this way I am less manipulated and less manipulating.

When I read Byron Katie's first book, *Loving What Is,* I was so taken with the simplicity and power of her teaching that I contacted her office. I discovered that she was married to one of my heroes, the poet Stephen Mitchell, and that they would both be in Los Angeles in a couple of weeks. I made an appointment to meet them, and spent the days before the meeting asking the four questions of every belief I held.

"I've been working with these questions nonstop for days," I said to Katie as we sat on the couch in her office, "and the fact is I cannot say with certainty that any of the beliefs I tell myself are true."

"And how does that make you feel?" she asked.

"Unbelievably free," I said. "Knowing I don't know is the greatest gift I have ever received."

"Do you absolutely know that to be true?" she asked. Of course I didn't, for that statement, too, was just another belief. The radical not-knowing that inquiry such as this offers is so liberating that it liberates us even from itself.

Not-knowing is the key to practicing truth. Not-knowing is different from doubting. Doubting assumes that I could know something to be true or false, but that I lack sufficient information to do so. Not-knowing is the realization of a psychospiritual version of the Heisenberg uncertainty principle.

In 1927 Werner Heisenberg postulated that in quantum physics one cannot precisely assign values for certain observable variables, such as position and momentum of a single particle at the same time. There are some things we just cannot, by the very nature of reality, know for certain. What Katie showed me is that the same is true of the beliefs I tell myself. I cannot know for certain if what I take to be so, is in fact so. Without the burden of certainty, I am free to engage life from a place of not-knowing, a place of radical curiosity and experimentation.

What happens when I do this? I take up my mat and walk on. I am no longer shackled by one system or another. I am free to learn from everyone and everything. Nothing is alien to me, and no idea is taboo. I feel myself loved by the infinite love that I call God's presence, and find that I become a conduit of that love in my dealings with others.

Whenever you find yourself acting from or even affirming to yourself and others your beliefs, stop and ask yourself these four questions, and allow the healing power of truth, the paradoxical truth of not-knowing, to free you from the paralysis of belief. And when you do so, you will find a bottomless well of lovingkindness feeding your spirit moment to moment.

PRESERVING KINDNESS FOR THE WORLD

Remembering and Retelling Tales of Kindness

Today I bent the truth to be kind, and I have no regret, for I am more sure of what is kind than I am of what is true.

—*Robert Brault*

Preserving kindness, the eighth of the Thirteen Attributes of Lovingkindness, speaks to what it means to be "you." It does so because its focus is on memory, thought, the stories we tell about ourselves and others—and we are nothing other than a collection of these memories, thoughts, and stories. To see what I mean by this, it helps to compare two classic teachings, one by Siddhartha Gautama, the sixth-century BCE Indian sage known as the Buddha, the Awakened One, and René Descartes, the seventeenth-century European philosopher.

All that we are is the result of what we have thought. In this opening line of the Dhammapada, one of the earliest collections of Buddhist teachings, the Buddha turns the much later saying of Descartes, "I think therefore I am" *(cogito ergo sum),* on its head. Descartes sought to find the one thing he could not doubt, and that turned out to be the fact that he was doubting in the first place. Doubt is a thought; thoughts require a thinker; hence, *I think therefore I am.* Buddha on the other hand places thought before the thinker; the thinker is the by-product of thought, and not the other way around.

Which is more accurate? Does the thinker produce the thought, or does the thought produce the thinker? It is a trick question, a koan, of sorts. And it was as a koan that I first encountered it.

I was living at an *ulpan,* an intensive Hebrew school and Israeli cultural boot camp, outside Jerusalem in the summer of 1976. One of my closest friends that summer was a fellow named Paul. Paul had two passions: becoming an Israeli paratrooper and studying Zen Buddhism. He discovered he could do both in Jerusalem, and he introduced me to a Zen master living in the Old City. Even though I often accompanied Paul on his visits to the master, and I was at the time serious about my own practice of *zazen,* Zen meditation, I cannot recall the master's name or even his nationality. All I remember is this one visit to his apartment in the Old City.

The apartment consisted of a bedroom, a kitchen, a bathroom, a living room set aside for meditation, and a small second bedroom for meeting students in *sanzen,* private interviews. Each room was sparsely furnished.

We sat cross-legged in *zazen* for about forty-five minutes and then went into the tiny kitchen for tea. As we sipped our tea, Paul brought up the question of Descartes's *cogito ergo sum* and Buddha's *You are what you think,* and asked *Sensei* (teacher) to comment.

"Nothing to say; no one to say it," *Sensei* said.

"Then who said that?" Paul asked with a straight face.

"Wrong question," *Sensei* said. "Right question is: Who said that?"

For a moment I thought *Sensei* and Paul were putting me on. This was so classic a Zen encounter that I doubted their sincerity. But it wasn't for show. *Sensei* was teaching and Paul was learning.

Sensei said, "Buddha and Descartes say same thing: I think I am. You big-paratrooper-Paul think you are, so you are, but only as long as you think. Stop thinking and Paul is gone."

"Dead?" I said for no good reason.

"Better than dead," *Sensei* replied. "Dead means you were born. No thought means no birth; no birth means no death. Dead can maybe come back, like Lazarus—you know that story? But no thought cannot come back because no thought never was."

"They can't both be right," Paul said. "Descartes said there is a thinker, Buddha said there is no thinker. They can't both be right."

"Descartes right. Buddha right. Paul wrong. Paul always wrong." *Sensei* laughed as he said this, and his laugh was contagious. The three of us laughed as we cleaned up the kitchen and returned to the living room to sit *zazen* for another half-hour or so.

We didn't stay long after the second sit, and as we walked to the bus stop to catch a bus back to the *ulpan*, I asked Paul if he understood what *Sensei* was saying about thoughts and thinkers.

"I got it," he said, "but I didn't really *get* it. You know what I mean? I see that there is no me without the thought of me, but I am still not certain as to who is thinking that thought."

"God is thinking that thought." Neither one of us had said that, so we turned around to see who had. An elderly Hasidic gentleman was sitting behind us at the bus stop. "Everything is in the mind of God," he said. "Everything is the thought of God. If God stops thinking you, you die. This is what it says in *Tanya*. You know *Tanya*, the *sefer* [book] of the Alter Rebbe?" The Alter Rebbe or Old Master is what Chabad Hasidim call their seventeenth-century founder, Rabbi Schneur Zalman of Liady.

The old man patted the empty bench on both sides of him, inviting us to sit down. "Always ready for more sitting with the master," Paul whispered more to himself than to me. Then he said to the Hasid, "Descartes said, *I think therefore I am*—he didn't posit a God because he could doubt the existence of God."

"And you already see the problem with his reasoning. Despite himself, Descartes assumes he is thinking the thought *I think therefore I am*. So his thinking is circular, and therefore it proves nothing."

"But you cannot prove God, either," Paul said.

"I don't have to prove God. God doesn't need me to prove God or believe in God. God doesn't need me at all. I need God. I need God for lots of reasons, but most importantly I need God to think the thought that is my very existence. So in a sense I could say, *I am, therefore God is*."

"Wait," I said. "Let me see if I get this. You are saying that we all exist as the thoughts of God. Since we exist, these thoughts exist, and since these thoughts exist, God exists. But that also presupposes something, namely God."

"Also circular reasoning," Paul said.

"True," the old man said. "Human thinking is always circular. We always end up proving the assumptions that generate the proofs. But that isn't the point. The point is that … Oh! Here is my bus."

This was all too much. Was this nameless Hasid simply going to ride off into the sunset without revealing the hidden secrets of Buddha and Descartes?

"Look," he said, as he laboriously lifted himself up the steps to get on the bus, "just ask yourself: Where do the thoughts come from?"

"The Buddhists say from emptiness, the void," Paul yelled as the man fished for coins for the bus.

"Emptiness, void, yes. The Alter Rebbe says God is *Ayin*, nothingness, the formless One in and from Whom all form emerges. So the Buddha was a Jew, who knew?" The door hissed closed and the conversation ended. As the bus growled down the street, Paul again broke into laughter. "A *Sensei* with *peyes* [side curls]," he said, "only in Jerusalem."

I think this story stayed with me because the issue is still very much on my mind. The phrase "You are what you think" is not as simple as it may at first appear.

Where are *you* when you accidentally but very violently stub your toe? Is there a *you* at that moment? There is sensation, painful in the extreme, but is there a *you* feeling the pain or is there just the pain?

I use this example because I just stubbed my toe a few minutes ago. At the moment of jamming the little toe of my right foot into the squat maple bookcase next to my desk, the pain overwhelmed any sense of self. I wasn't in pain; there was just pain. As the pain faded, *I* emerged, feeling both angry and foolish, and looking for someone to blame for my clumsiness.

So there can be awareness without an *I* that is aware. When I stubbed my toe, there was acute awareness of pain, but no one to be aware of it. The *I* that registers the sensation as pain comes after the fact of the pain. The *I* is a by-product of the sensation, allowing me to have the feeling of pain by inventing a *me* that was in pain. My own experience proves that there was no *me* in pain; there was just pain. The *me* comes afterward. The *me,* the *I* always comes afterward, or, better yet, after word.

This is more than just a pun. This is key to understanding Buddha, Descartes, and the Alter Rebbe. There is no *you* without thought. There is no thought without words—sensation, yes, but not thought. You are a linguistic creation, no less than Sherlock Holmes or Harry Potter. They exist only in the stories told about them. The same is true of you and me.

When the story ceases, we cease: no birth, no death. Or, to paraphrase the Buddha, "All that you are is the story you tell." And since the story you tell is always a patchwork quilt of past thoughts and memories, we can also say that you are what you remember. And because you are what you remember, memory becomes a key component in the cultivation of lovingkindness. If your stories are kind, you will be kind and bring kindness to the world. If your stories are cruel, you will be cruel and bring suffering to the world.

The stories we tell are the stuff of memory. Memory is a habit of mind, another way to build and sustain our sense of identity. And we preserve memory through story. When you remember an especially fine meal you shared with a close friend, you do not recall the event as if you were making a PowerPoint presentation:

- Date, time, and place of meeting.
- Purpose of meeting.
- Foods eaten; beverages consumed.
- Topics discussed: family, troubles at work, future expectations.

If you are recounting the event to someone else, you tell a story:

Jack and I met at the Northside Deli for dinner that night. He was a little late because of a last-minute rewrite of an article due that day. It was great to just relax and talk. I shared with him …

If you are recalling the event in your own mind for yourself alone, you replay it as you remember it, much as you would watch a show on television. You are what you remember, and what you remember are stories.

Who would you be if you lost your memory and forgot all your stories? Who would you be if you awoke tomorrow morning without any memory of your name, age, relationships, job, and past? What would be the first thing you would do?

I have asked this of my students over the past few years. Most believe that with or without memory they would still be themselves. Most say they would check through personal (or rather assumed personal) artifacts to find the phone number of someone who could tell them who they were, what they did, and whether they mattered to anyone else. And with that person's help, they would try to rebuild the memory that was lost.

This is not surprising. In fact, this is what we do every day. Every day, all day, we turn to someone, usually memory itself, to remind us who we are and why we matter. This is neither good nor bad; this is simply what we do. And, knowing that this is what we do, we must ask the question: Which memories do we use to build the self we imagine ourselves to be?

So ask yourself, what do you remember? What memories are the building blocks of your self? Here are some of mine: I remember I am a Jew, an American, a rabbi, a father, a husband, and a son. There are many more memories than these, but these will do. Each of these memories comes with a story, and each of these stories, woven together, defines who I am. My entire life is predicated on the truths I extrapolate from my stories.

I am a Jew means that I am more interested in things Jewish than in things Hindu. *I am a Jew* means I am part of a people with its own set of values and beliefs. *I am a Jew* means that Israel matters to me more than Denmark. *I am a Jew* means that I have a certain past that colors my present and shapes my destiny. *I am a Jew* means that anti-Semitism is my problem. *I am a Jew* means I am concerned about what it is to be a Jew. I could go on, but I trust that the idea is clear.

The same kind of thing happens with other facts taken from my stories. You are what you remember. What you remember is your story. Your story is your self.

Given all this, you can see why preserving kindness is one of the Thirteen Attributes of Lovingkindness: By remembering and retelling tales of kindness, we create a self that is loving and kind.

OUR STORIES, OUR SELVES

What stories do you tell yourself about yourself? What stories about yourself do you tell others? Most of us have a few powerful stories that we tell to new people we meet and with whom we wish to develop a relationship. Think back to times when you were sitting with a stranger you hoped would become a friend. What stories did you tell about yourself? What information did you convey? What do these stories say about you?

Most of us have no idea what stories we tell, and no idea what these stories are saying about us. When we carefully examine these stories, many of us find that we tell stories of pain and suffering, stories that feed a negative image of self. Many people tell less than flattering stories to lower expectations about themselves, or to gain some leverage with the other person by playing a game of negative one-upmanship. If I can prove that I am more of a victim than you, I can use that to excuse my negative behavior while holding you to a higher standard.

When I listen to the stories I tell, I discover that I tend to tell self-deprecating stories. Why? I suspect it is reflective of an ancient Jewish habit of warding off evil by avoiding words of praise. Whenever my Russian *bubbe* (grandmother) would say something nice about someone she would quickly, albeit lightly, spit three times, saying *K'ayin harah!* which is Yiddish for "May the Evil Eye not curse you for your happiness." I don't spit, but I tend to play down the praise in hopes of avoiding the Evil Eye.

I rarely tell stories of kindness. I tend to remember slights— those I have made and those I have received. The more I tell such stories, the more I become the stories I tell. I had to work on shifting my storytelling to include at least some tales of kindness. And while I do that much more than I used to, a careful examination of my tales still shows that I tell such stories far more often about other people than about myself. I am not saying I don't do acts of kindness; I am saying that I tend not to preserve these acts in the stories I tell. And since I am the stories I tell, I fail to reinforce kindness by failing to tell those stories.

PRESERVING KINDNESS THROUGH AN ETHICAL WILL

How do we preserve kindness? We preserve kindness the way we preserve any other value we cherish—we tell stories about it. Preserving kindness means telling stories of lovingkindness from your past, but not only your personal past. Working this attribute means exploring your family history to find stories of lovingkindness. Talk with relatives and explore your collective memories to sift out these tales. They may be small incidents of kindness that went largely unnoticed at the time, but which, in hindsight, are the stuff of kindness tales. When you find these stories, share them. The more you tell them, the more kindness will take root.

One of the best ways to practice preserving kindness is to create an ethical will. Writing an ethical will is a centuries-old Jewish practice that is making a comeback among Jews and others. Originally an oral tradition, with parents passing on their values, blessings, life lessons, and forgiveness to their children, ethical wills have been committed to writing for the past one thousand years.

> An ethical will is not an easy thing to write. In doing so, one confronts oneself. One must look inward to see what are the essential truths one has learned in a lifetime, face up to one's failures, and consider what are the things that really count. Thus an individual learns a great deal about himself or herself when writing an ethical will.[1]

Although there is no wrong way to write an ethical will, it may be of help to you to follow an outline. Here is one that I have used with people in the past:

1. Begin by clarifying to whom your ethical will is addressed. You may choose to write a separate will for different people. Whomever you decide to write to, open the will as you would a letter: "Dear ..." In fact, think of the will as a letter and write it in a conversational style.

2. Open with a brief statement of your core values and beliefs. It may be humility and kindness, or creativity and daring, or care for others, or some combination of these and other values. The purpose here is to let readers know what values you are bequeathing to them. The rest of your ethical will explores these values through personal stories.

3. Now tell your stories. How did you first learn about kindness or compassion? What happened? How did the experience shape you? If you are telling a story as part of an ethical will, it is most likely a story that has great significance for you, so don't rush the telling or ignore the implications of the story for your life. One story may lead to another and then another. While you don't want to overdo it, there is no reason to limit yourself to only one story per value.

4. Once your stories have been written down, you might consider sharing some of your hopes for your loved one's future. The challenge here is to keep the will values-focused and not behavior-focused. In other words, this is not the place to burden your child with your wish that she become a heart surgeon when she is passionate about art history and has no interest at all in medicine. All that accomplishes is stirring up feelings of guilt. If you wish to speak to your hopes for the future, stick to the values that matter to you.

5. Close your ethical will with words of forgiveness. If there are things you wish you had done and didn't do

for the person receiving the will, ask for forgiveness. If there were things not said that should have been said, write them here and apologize for waiting so long to express them. If there were things said or done that you wish you had not said or done, admit to these as well, and ask for forgiveness. The tone of the closing section of your ethical will should be one of deep compassion for both yourself and the person to whom you are writing. No excuses are necessary here. Simply speak the truth with all humility, and offer forgiveness along with your love.

While some people choose to write their ethical will, others find writing uncomfortable and prefer to tape-record it instead. Before he died, Mark Lodner, a dear friend and an accomplished broadcast journalist, used his computer to record his ethical will on a CD. I played the recording at his funeral. Just prior to the closing prayer, we all sat silently as he spoke to us "from beyond the grave," sharing his deepest truths, giving thanks to those he loved, asking for forgiveness from those he may have hurt, and offering forgiveness to all of us. It was one of the most moving moments I have ever experienced, and one that made the value of creating an ethical will crystal clear.

Your will need not be written all at once. You can begin by collecting stories, jotting them down, and storing them in a safe place. Slowly, you can turn these jottings into teaching tales for your ethical will. You can, of course, share them as you write them—just don't neglect to collect them all in one place and put them in a readable form. Over time you will produce a solid piece of work that can be passed on to loved ones. This is preserving kindness for the world.

CHAPTER NINE

FEELINGS AND FORGIVENESS

Forgiving Iniquity, Forgiving Willfulness, Forgiving Error

Forgiveness is better than revenge.
—*Diogenes Laertius,* Pittacus, Iii

Forgiveness and lovingkindness are inextricably bound to each other. Lovingkindness that is not grounded in forgiveness is not true lovingkindness. Forgiveness not grounded in lovingkindness is not true forgiveness.

Forgiveness is not forgetting, excusing, accepting, denying, or numbing yourself to pain. If someone hurts you, it is unreasonable to think that you can just forget it and move on. Forgetting is not a matter of will. You cannot forget on command. Neither can you will yourself not to feel hurt when a hurtful act is recalled. Nor would it be wise to do so.

Jorge Santayana's aphorism, "Those who forget the past are doomed to relive it," is applicable here. When it comes to forgiveness, memory is not your enemy, though obsessing over memories may be. It is one thing to remember that the last time you touched a hot stove you got burned; it is another to avoid stoves altogether.

So forgiveness is not forgetting; you can use what you know about the past to live more constructively in the present.

Neither is forgiveness excusing. Even if you know the reason that a wrongful act was committed, that reason does not excuse it. No matter what drama underlies your behavior, it is always your choice to engage in that behavior. You cannot excuse yourself for abusing another because you yourself were abused. You cannot excuse yourself for drinking today because you drank yesterday. The past tells us where we were, and what we did, but does not lock us into staying there and endlessly repeating the same hurtful behaviors.

Forgiveness isn't acceptance, if by acceptance you mean acquiescing to an ongoing hurtful, unjust, or dangerous situation. You should never accept the pain and suffering others inflict on you, or the pain and suffering you inflict on others. You need to confront the situation that causes the pain and change it. So acceptance as surrender is not forgiveness.

Forgiveness isn't denial. If you have done something horrible, or if something horrible has or is being done to you, the first step toward forgiveness is recognizing that something horrible has occurred. Denial gets you nowhere. You must accept that reality is reality, and that there is no need to pretend that things are other than they are.

There is one other thing that forgiveness is not: numbing. There are people who pretend to feel no pain. They claim to be so rooted in spacious mind that they rise above the suffering experienced by narrow mind. They see this as a sign of spiritual maturity. When they inflict pain on others, they respond to the other's pain by blaming their victim for a lack of spiritual depth. People who claim that spacious mind is impervious to suffering know nothing about spacious mind. What they are calling spacious mind is in fact narrow mind, numbed by fear and sorrow.

Spacious mind feels everything; it simply clings to nothing. Spacious mind allows all feelings to arise, notes and learns from those feelings, and then allows them to fade. Feelings come and go. They fade over time. Narrow mind tries to avoid those feelings it dislikes and cling to those it does like. Spacious mind clings to nothing and has room for everything. Someone who claims to be so holy as to feel no emotional pain is mistaking holiness for callousness. The truly holy feel everyone's pain; they just don't hold on to it.

If forgiveness isn't forgetting, excusing, accepting, denying, or numbing, then what is it? Forgiveness is letting go. Letting go means that you do not cling to memories and feelings.

There are certain memories of past behaviors that haunt me. Whenever they arise my stomach churns, my palms sweat, and my head aches. I feel physically and emotionally rotten. These are things for which I have yet to forgive myself, even if others have forgiven me for them.

You might read this and say, "Good! You should feel sick over the terrible things you have done." My response to this is "Why?"

Let me be as clear as I can about this. When I first confront something awful that I have done, I do feel terrible. That is an appropriate response. My guilt and shame are ways my feelings make clear to me that I have done something wrong. Once I have grasped this, however, these feelings are useless. What I have to do is turn my attention to making amends, but if the feelings are my focus I will make them the center of attention, and never get around to making amends.

We assume that feelings are motivators, and that nothing gets done until we feel like doing it. We make ourselves servants of our feelings and use feelings to excuse both action and inaction. But this is just one more false belief we tell ourselves.

Many years ago I was hired as a leadership coach by a CEO of a small graphic arts company in Chicago. Anger was one of the issues we worked on. During one of our meetings together she took a phone call from her daughter that made her so angry she slammed down the phone, picked up a framed photo of her daughter that had been sitting on her desk, and was about to throw it against the wall when her secretary knocked and stepped into the office. After an almost imperceptible moment of hesitation, the secretary told the CEO that she had to take another call from an important customer. The CEO put the picture down, picked up the phone, dealt politely with the customer, and then hung up the phone. For a moment I thought all was well, but when she noticed the picture of her daughter lying faceup on her desk, the anger returned, and she grabbed the photo and smashed it against the wall.

"I am so mad at my daughter, I can't help myself!" she said to me by way of apology.

"You helped yourself when you were talking to your customer," I said. "Where did your anger go while you were on that phone call?"

She thought about that for a moment and said, "I don't know where it went. It was just gone. I was thinking about what this guy was saying and trying to solve his problem, and I guess I forgot I was angry. But when I saw that photo I remembered and got angry again."

"Makes sense," I said. "But it doesn't explain throwing the picture. The feeling of anger doesn't explain the throwing of the photograph; it only precedes it. Sure you were angry, and you may get angry every time you think about whatever it was that your daughter said that made you angry in the first place, but throwing the picture was a choice. You wanted to throw the picture, so you threw it. Then you wanted to explain why you threw it, so you grasped on to the anger and claimed temporary insanity. I don't buy it."

Feelings do not justify or excuse behavior. Feelings simply tell you how another person's behavior is impacting you, and vice versa. Just imagine if you ran your life according to your feelings. What would happen to you if you acted on every feeling that entered your conscious mind? You would end up in a mental institution. Chances are you are not reading this book while residing in such an institution, so chances are you do not allow your feelings to dictate your behavior, only to scapegoat it.

If you can't use your feelings to excuse new behavior, why use them to continually berate yourself for past behavior? You have done some awful things in your life—things that you will regret until the day you die. You can't forget those things or ignore how wrong they were. But to continually return to the feelings of guilt and shame whenever these things pop into your mind is useless. All that matters is that you make amends and not repeat the mistake again. Beating yourself up is just histrionic excess, part of the drama that distracts you—as it did the paralytic in the Gospels—from the realization of forgiveness. As long as you focus on yourself and your feelings, you will never get around to making amends and letting go; you will never get around to forgiveness.

LEARNING TO LET GO THROUGH *NAMA-JAPA*

It is easy to say you should let go of your feelings once you have felt them, but actually doing this isn't quite so easy. How can you let go? There are, no doubt, many methods, but the one I find the most helpful is called *nama-japa,* repetition of a Name of God. The term *nama-japa* is Sanskrit and refers to the Hindu practice of silently repeating a mantra over and over as a means of returning over and again to spacious mind. Every religion has its own version of *nama-japa.* In Hebrew it is called *gerushin,* from *l'garish,* to divorce or separate. By repeating a Name of God over and over, you separate yourself from the drama that is swirling around and within you.

The practice is simple. Find a Name of God or some other short word or phrase that speaks to you of spacious mind and consciously repeat it all day long. Of course you will forget periodically during the day, and when you notice that you have forgotten, just start up again. Practicing *nama-japa* this way is like exercising a muscle. When you need to free yourself from a compulsive thought, feeling, or even action, directing your full attention to the repetition will allow you to let the compulsivity go.

Here are some of the most common mantras. Experiment with these or find others. When you find one that works—that is, one you can repeat effortlessly—make that your master key for unlocking the chains of compulsivity.

- Allah
- *HaRachaman* (Compassionate One)
- Jesus
- Ram
- *Om*
- *Shalom/Salaam*
- Peace
- *Maranatha* (Come, Lord)

Once you have a means of working with the compulsive nature of not-forgiving, you can begin to focus on the three types of sin we are to forgive. While the act of forgiveness is the same for each sin, the fact that there are three different types of sin—iniquity, willfulness, and error, or missing the mark—causes each act of forgiveness to be listed as a separate attribute of lovingkindness: numbers ten, eleven, and twelve, respectively. We will take up each in turn.

FORGIVING INIQUITY

Iniquity is gross injustice; it is an act of premeditated exploitation. You have done something to benefit yourself at the expense of another. The means is most often deceit. You lied about yourself or a situation, and allowed the other person to make decisions based on faulty information.

How do you forgive gross injustice? For simplicity's sake, I will address this as if you were seeking forgiveness rather than bestowing it. To do the latter, simply adjust this conversation accordingly.

First, you admit that the injustice happened. Second, you do what you can to correct it and make amends. Third, you allow yourself to feel the shame and guilt your conscience improves without defense or drama. And fourth, you let the drama go.

Let those memories of iniquity come to you in full force. Write them down in a journal in detail. Pay special attention to how the other person responded when the pain of your action was felt. Begin with the physical. What was the person's body language? How did the shock and pain manifest themselves in his body? Be specific. In this way you will have a more difficult time pretending that the pain you caused wasn't that bad.

Now move on to the emotional level. What feelings did your actions evoke? Don't settle for the obvious: anger. Note the anger and then look more deeply. Look for the sadness; for the loss of self-esteem; for the loss of trust. See how the other person turned on himself, compounding his pain by blaming himself for what you did.

Shift your focus to the level of story, the intellect. What story did you shatter in the other? What damaging story did you plant in him? In what way have you infected his sense of what is real with a sense of unreality? In what way have you robbed him of hope, trust, and safety?

As you follow these steps, you will feel horrible. If you don't, you are either picking on something for which you have already received forgiveness, or you are hiding in the false spaciousness of numbness.

Feel bad. It won't kill you. Use these feelings as a catalyst to make amends, as long as doing so doesn't inflict more pain. Do something positive that will help offset the damage you have caused. After you have done all you can do by way of making amends, and have learned all you can learn from what you did, make a solemn vow not to repeat the act.

Assuming you have done all this, let it go. How? The next time the memory arises, don't give yourself over to the drama. "Yes, I did that. I won't do that again. There is no point in dwelling on it, and doing so simply feeds my narcissism. Better to do something constructive with my time and energy."

The Hasidim have a saying: "No matter how you stir a pot of filth it is always a pot of filth. Better to let the pot be, and string pearls for the sake of heaven." The pot of filth is past iniquity; stirring it is losing yourself in the narcissistic drama of your past. Stirring up the past only distracts you from the opportunity to do good in the present: stringing pearls for the sake of heaven.

FORGIVING WILLFULNESS

Willfulness is forcing or manipulating people into doing what you want done when it is not in their best interest to do so. The difference between iniquity and willfulness is that with iniquity you are deliberately doing something to harm another, while with willfulness you are simply trying to help yourself at another's expense. You may not wish or intend the other harm, but the hurt happens as a by-product of you helping yourself.

Willfulness can be done overtly or covertly. It can be done from a position of strength or from a position of weakness. You can force people to bend to your will, and you can shame people into bending to your will. Some people are such masters of willfulness that their victims do not even know they are being manipulated.

Willfulness is always about manipulation, bullying, getting your own way. While you may be subtle in being willful, there is nothing subtle about willfulness itself. Hold up a mirror to your actions and look to see ways in which you are forcing people to acquiesce to your will and desire. Once you see that you are doing this, stop doing it.

This is simple, but in no way easy. You aren't manipulating people for the mere fun of it. You are doing so to protect yourself in some way. If you don't get people to do what you want, you are afraid that you will never get what you need. Willfulness is rooted in a fearful lack of self-esteem.

At the heart of willfulness is the story of your own unworthiness. People would never be kind to you if you didn't shame them into it. People would never be of help to you if you didn't trick them into it. People would never follow you if you didn't bully them into it. And once guilt, trickery, and bullying become habitual, they reinforce the story of your own unworthiness and make freeing yourself from willfulness very difficult.

The key to forgiving willfulness is to uproot the story that supports it. Willfulness is rooted in your sense of being unloved and unlovable. This is a delusion. God's love is unconditional; it cannot be earned or lost.

This is difficult for some people to accept. They are so invested in being unloved that they cannot bear to see themselves as worthy of love. Simply ask to be shown God's love, and then keep your eyes open to seeing it. Look for the gifts of grace you receive from God (or the universe) through the deeds and words of other beings. Review the answers to your *Naikan* question "What did others do for me today?" and realize that you are loved by perfect strangers. The more you find that you are loved, the less you will feel the need to manipulate people into loving you. The more you discover that you are loved, the more love you will attract, and the more you will love others in turn.

FORGIVING ERROR

Error, *chata'ah* in Hebrew, comes from a Hebrew archery term meaning "to miss one's target." You have a target, a goal, an intention. You take careful aim and loose your arrow, your word or deed, and you miss. The miss was accidental. You just missed. It happens; no matter how well you plan, no matter how loving your intention, there are times when things just go wrong.

Forgiving these accidental and unintended errors is the twelfth of the Thirteen Attributes of Lovingkindness. They are easily forgiven by others, but sometimes not so easily by yourself. You know this to be so: Someone hurts you inadvertently, and, knowing it was an accident, you let the hurt go. You do not spin a drama around it. It happened, you felt hurt, it passed, and you moved on.

While you can easily forgive others for the inadvertent hurts they may cause you, you may have trouble forgiving yourself for the accidental hurts you cause others. There may be lots of reasons for this, but all of them come down to narcissism. If you cannot accept the fact that you sometimes make mistakes, then you are too wrapped up in the delusion of your own perfection.

When you cannot let go, even when the injured party has forgiven you, you can be fairly certain that it is your belief about the sin and not the sin itself that is the problem.

MAIMONIDES' FIVEFOLD PATH TO FORGIVENESS

The twelfth-century Jewish sage Maimonides taught a five-stage practice of forgiveness called *teshuvah,* turning (*Mishneh Torah, Hilchos Teshuvah* 2:2):

1. **Pay attention.** Recognize that you are acting in a hurtful way, and cease doing that action immediately. This means that you have to watch yourself, you have to cultivate the witness that is spacious mind and pay attention to what narrow mind is doing and saying. Repeating your mantra is one way of doing this. As soon as you realize that you are acting or speaking inappropriately, stop.

2. **Feel regret.** See the pain and suffering you are causing and allow yourself to feel bad about it. This leads to the desire to renounce that behavior in the future. Until we fully feel the pain we cause, and fully commit to changing this behavior, there is no hope of turning.

Steps 1 and 2 are internal, private, and as such they are somewhat easy. Steps 3 and 4 are external, interpersonal, and much more difficult. Lots of people who wrestle with turning stop after step 2, imagining that "willing makes it so." It doesn't. Nothing can be done without the will, but will alone—internal conviction without external behavior—is not enough.

3. **Confess.** Verbalize your regret out loud. It is important that you speak aloud, that you hear what it is you are saying. Doing so makes the act of confession and contrition real. It is too easy to gloss over a problem when you only admit it to yourself. Admitting a failing to another makes it more real, less easy to evade or sugarcoat. You can express your regret to a trusted friend, partner, spouse, counselor, therapist, or clergyperson. But share it with someone.

4. **Ask forgiveness and reconcile.** The *Mishnah*, the early anthology of rabbinic teachings, says, "For transgressions against God, the Day of Atonement atones. But for transgressions of one human being against another, the Day of Atonement does not atone until they have made peace with one another." The Day of Atonement, Yom Kippur, is, next to Shabbat, the holiest day of the Jewish year, yet it is ineffectual when it comes to making peace between people. God can forgive you for the sins you commit against yourself and God, but God cannot forgive you for the pain you

cause others unless and until you first ask them for forgiveness.

Regret and confession are not enough. You have to confront the person you have wronged and ask for forgiveness. This is the ultimate act of humbling oneself, of opening narrow mind to the healing of spacious mind. The Jewish tradition says that if you sincerely ask a person for forgiveness three times and they still refuse to forgive you, then God intervenes and you are forgiven. But you have to ask first.

5. **Plan ahead.** To avoid repeating this hurtful behavior, look ahead and see when you may well find yourself in a position to do that same thing again. Maimonides taught that you never know you have truly turned until you find yourself in a similar situation, yet acting differently than before. Prepare for this in advance. Imagine scenarios that will trigger the negative response you are trying to avoid, and come up with alternative ways of dealing with the situation. Visualize yourself taking these alternatives paths. In this way they will be waiting for you if and when the need arises.

Maimonides' five-step process isn't easy, but it works. All you have to do is try it.

CHAPTER TEN

CLEANSING DELUSION TO SEE CLEARLY

Recognizing Manifestations of God

Be your sins like crimson, they can turn snow-white;
be they wool dyed scarlet, they can become like pure
white fleece.

—*Isaiah 1:18*

You cannot be kind if your understanding is clouded. Loving-kindness demands clarity of vision. It is only when you see what is that you can engage it lovingly. What is it that you see? That you and your neighbor, that you and all things, are one in, with, and as God. Cleansing delusion, the last of the Thirteen Attributes of Lovingkindness, is all about seeing clearly.

Imagine two identical twins. They are in their mid-twenties and, so you are told, exceptionally beautiful young women. When either one walks down the street, people literally stop and stare. Now imagine that these twins are facing you, standing about ten feet in front of you. Each of them is covered in a thick layer of mud. The mud is so thick that you cannot make out their features. While you have been told that these are two of the most beautiful people in the world, you cannot verify that for yourself.

Now imagine that a light shower of pure rain is falling on one of them, slowly washing the mud away from the one while the other is still caked from head to toe. As the rain dissolves the mud from the one twin, you begin to see the beauty of which you have heard. With the washing away of the last of the mud, you stand in awe of this perfect form. Yet, even though you believe the mud-covered twin is just as beautiful, try as you will you cannot conjure up the same feelings of awe for the mud-covered twin as for the rain-washed twin.

You are like these twins. You are a perfect image of the One True Reality, God, Brahman, Tao, Dharmakaya, Allah. Chances are, however, that when you look in a mirror you do not see the Image of God, but rather a mud-caked heap of attractions, repulsions, hungers, thirsts, and passions.

So you engage in any number of bathing rituals to wash away the mud. You join this or that religion, follow this or that guru, and devote yourself to this or that practice in hopes of scraping off the mud and uncovering your true self. But nothing changes. It is like stopping at a red light and having someone rush out to "wash" your windshield with a filthy rag. The dirt is moved but not removed. Real cleansing, the cleansing that is the Thirteenth Attribute of Lovingkindness, is not a matter of changing from one state into another, but of realizing that all states are part of God's manifest reality. You are not cleansed of desire; you are cleansed of the delusion that you need to be.

One morning while I was studying Zen Buddhism as an undergraduate at Smith College, my professor, Taitetsu Unno, taught us the story of how Hui Neng, an illiterate Chinese monk, became the Sixth Patriarch of Chan, the Chinese source of Japanese Zen.

To choose his successor, the Fifth Patriarch held a contest. He challenged his monks to express their understanding of reality in a poem. The author who best expressed an understanding of the Buddha nature, what I am calling spacious mind, would become the Sixth Patriarch. The monks knew that only Shen Hsiu, the head monk, could write such a poem, so it was only he who submitted one. Shen Hsiu wrote:

> The body is the wisdom tree; the mind a mirror bright.
> Take care to wipe it all the time, and let no dust alight.

Although the Fifth Patriarch praised Shen Hsiu's poem, he was not satisfied.

Hui Neng had no standing in the community, and could not write a word. So he had another monk write this poem for him and nailed it to the wall next to Shen Hsiu's poem:

> There is no tree of wisdom, nor mind or mirror bright.
> Since all is empty from the first, on what can dust alight?

The Fifth Patriarch read Hui Neng's poem and knew immediately that he was destined to be the Sixth Patriarch. Fearing that the other monks would resent him and perhaps kill him, the Fifth Patriarch derided Hui Neng's poem in public. In the middle of the night, however, he summoned Hui Neng to him, gave him the transmission, robe, and bowl of the Patriarch and urged him to flee to the South and remain incognito until it was safe for him to reveal himself and begin teaching.

Later that day I wrote my own response to both Shen Hsiu and Hui Neng, and taped it on the door to Professor Unno's office:

> Since there is no wisdom tree or mirror polished bright,
> And since all is empty from morning through the night,
> Tell me from whence this dust does come that all fear will
>   alight?

While I had no pretense to enlightenment, I did feel that the Fifth Patriarch let Hui Neng off a bit too easy. When I asked

Professor Unno to comment on my poem, he, like the Fifth Patriarch, did not publicly applaud my spiritual insight. In fact, he found it pedantic and derivative. No matter, I fully expected him to call me into his office that evening and privately give me his robe and bowl. He didn't.

Enlightenment aside, if everything is God, and I believe it is, then the dust on the mirror and the mud on the twins are no less divine than polished glass and rain-washed bodies. The true cleansing is not the removal of anything, but the seeing into the true nature of everything.

The mud, the stains, the errors—the hurtful, foolish, and maddening things you have done in your life—are no less manifestations of God than the just, kind, and humble acts you have performed. And until you realize this, you are trapped in an exhaustive effort to be someone other than yourself. This act of psychospiritual violence makes true lovingkindness impossible for two reasons. First, because it puts off being kind until you have understood yourself better. Second, because it creates a state of inner turmoil that generates anger and frustration rather than kindness and love.

Jesus says, "Be perfect as your heavenly Father is perfect" (Matthew 5:48). In this case perfect doesn't mean without blemish; it means to be whole and complete. God tells us through the prophet Isaiah, "I form light and create darkness, I make good and create evil; I, the One Who Is, do all these things" (Isaiah 45:7). God's perfection includes darkness and evil. To be whole, God must be everything and its opposite. And if we are to be whole as God is whole, then we too must take ownership of duality as an expression of our greater nonduality.

If you know all is God, then you love the mud-caked twin as well as the rain-washed twin. You don't make the distinction between mud and no mud, between dust and no dust. Mud is God, and dust is God; just as no mud is God, and no dust is God. I am not saying that you do not make distinctions between mud and no mud, but that you do not imagine that one is God and the other not. And what is the delusion from which we must be cleansed? The delusion that we must be cleansed at all!

I was once teaching a Sunday-school class at a synagogue in Taos, New Mexico. I took the kids outside so we could look at the mountains surrounding us. I told them how much I loved mountains, how in awe I was just looking at them, and I bemoaned the fact that we had to waste space between the mountains with valleys.

"Wouldn't it be great," I said, "if we could fill in the valleys with other mountains?"

For a moment the kids said nothing, then they laughed. One said, "That makes no sense. If you fill in the valleys with mountains, everything would be flat. You need the valleys in order to have the mountains."

Smart kids. Mountains without valleys, crests without troughs, good without evil, light without dark—these make no sense. Each goes with the other. They are not the same—no one would mistake a valley for a mountain—but neither are they separate and apart. They are part of a duality within a greater nonduality.

You have the capacity for kindness and the capacity for cruelty. Each goes with the other. And to try to rid yourself of the latter in order to cultivate the former is an act of self-destruction that only adds to the violence of our world. This is why the Psalmist wrote, "Turn from evil and do good" (Psalm 34:15) rather than "put an end to evil and do good." You cannot put an end to evil, for evil and good go together like trough and crest, but you can turn from it and do something else—something good.

So much of what passes for spirituality ties you to the delusion that you must be other than you are to be better than you have been. This is nonsense. You cannot be other than you are. And who you are now is not exactly who you were a moment ago, let alone months or years ago. Even if you imitate your past and allow yourself to fall into habitual patterns of behavior, each replication is in and of itself a new action.

I don't believe in habits. I believe in unconscious acts, and I believe in laziness. Much of what passes for habit is simply unconscious behavior. And much of that is neither good nor bad, though it may or may not be constructive. Once you are aware of a habit, however, it is no longer unconscious; it can be brought under your control. Behavior, unlike cravings, thoughts, feelings, and addictions, is within your power to control. If you choose not to control a behavior that you wish you no longer had, do not chalk this up to powerlessness, but to laziness.

At this point my Twelve-Step friends may be up in arms. The First Step says that we admit to being unable to control whatever addiction we suffer from. As a member of Overeaters Anonymous, I know this to be true. I am powerless over certain foods. But all that means is that I cannot wrench myself free from my addiction. I cannot will myself to be other than myself. So I approach it another way. I surrender the addiction to God. When I am caught in the trap of addiction, I do not try to wrestle free. Instead, I surrender to God and ask God to handle the craving for me. In other words, I shift from narrow mind to spacious mind and allow things to follow their course. And when I do, I don't overeat. The craving may remain, but the compulsion to give in to it is gone. I didn't defeat my addiction; I turned from it.

If you wait until you are perfect, in the sense of being free from all negativity, before you engage in lovingkindness, you will never engage in lovingkindness. And thinking you have to change is the delusion that makes change impossible. What do you do, then? Turn and drop the whole thing.

CLEANSING DELUSION THROUGH TURNING

How do you turn? There is no how—there is just turning. I know this sounds silly, but it is true. You do not prepare to turn, or engage in some other action that will help you to turn; you turn. If you find yourself behaving in a manner you know to be harmful to yourself and/or others, just turn away from it. If it helps to take a moment and offer the behavior up to God, say something like, "God, please take this behavior from me for the moment so that I might do something else," and then do something else. Don't wait to feel differently. Don't wait to be sure that God has removed the problem. Just do something else.

I feel a bit like Nancy Reagan, saying, "Just say no," but I truly believe that the key to turning is turning. Anything I might add feeds back into the delusion that you must be mud-free before you can be holy. Not so. The mud is God, too.

The more you turn, the more you see the divinity of the mud. The more you see the true nature of the mud, the more kind and compassionate you become regarding yourself and your addictions. The more compassion you have for yourself, the more you will have for others.

THE GREATEST OBSTACLE
TO LOVINGKINDNESS

Anger blows out the light of the mind.
—*Robert G. Ingersoll*

The greatest block to lovingkindness is anger. Anger is what happens when narrow mind doesn't get its way. This was true when you were two years old, and it is true today. When things go your way, you are not angry. But when they do not go your way, anger is often your first response.

Laura Huxley, in a delightful book called *You Are Not the Target*, offers this parable:

> You are canoeing on a lake. You are relaxed, happy, and at peace with yourself and your world. As you paddle around, you notice that a fog is rolling in and you decide it is time to head toward shore. As you do so, another canoe appears nearby. It too is heading toward the shore. Unfortunately, it is doing so along a trajectory that will cause it to ram your canoe in the process. You call out to the other canoe, warning of the danger. You steer your canoe this way and that trying to avoid the other boat, but no matter what you do the other canoe seems intent on

ramming you. You are getting frightened, and not a little angry. This other fellow must be a fool or worse, and you shout out that fact loudly and often. Yet the canoe continues to stalk you, and with a great bang and shudder it hits you hard. By this point you are ready to physically attack the other, but as you peer through the fog you discover that there is no one paddling the canoe. It had simply come loose from its moorings and rammed into you through no fault of its own. You realize you were not the target, and all of sudden your anger is gone.[1]

There are at least two lessons to be gleaned from Huxley's story. First, that anger requires you to be the target. Second, that when you realize you are not the target, it simply and immediately disappears. Where does the anger go?

To be honest, I have no idea. I have experienced the sudden vanishing of anger many times, but I cannot say where the anger goes. Perhaps it would help if we knew where the anger came from in the first place.

Some people claim that anger rests in the unconscious. I don't know how anyone could know this, however. The whole point of the unconscious is that it is not conscious, and therefore it is impossible for the conscious mind to know what is in the unconscious. Anger may be there or it may not be there, but as long as the unconscious is unconscious we have no way of knowing one way or the other. If we don't know but continue to theorize that this is so, we are simply trapped in a belief.

Other people believe that anger is held in the skeletal structure of the body. Indeed, when I am angry I can see manifestations of that anger in my body: My heart races, my stomach tightens, my breathing gets shallow. But when I am not experiencing anger, I cannot find it in my body any more than I can find it in my mind.

It seems to me that anger resides in neither the body nor the mind, but in the story. If you knew that the canoe about to ram you were simply adrift, you might feel fear, imagining that you could capsize on impact, but you wouldn't necessarily feel anger. Anger requires a story that makes you a target. When you imagine that you are a target, you get angry; otherwise, you don't.

I said a moment ago that anger happens when you do not get what you want. That was only half the story. If you buy a lottery ticket hoping to win a million dollars, you may be disappointed when you don't win, but not angry. Anger requires the additional element of being a target. If you discover (or even come to believe falsely) that the lottery is rigged against you, then you become angry. Listen to the stories you tell about yourself when you are angry. If you listen carefully, you will find that at the heart of your anger is the notion that you are somehow the target.

Anger is one way for you to keep yourself at the center of the story. After all, you matter so much that "they" are out to get you. This is why anger is so addictive: It literally keeps you going. As Buddhist teacher Robert Thurman writes,

> Anger is a deadly sin, a destructive addiction, and a major cause of crime and death—but only when its fiery energy is misdirected by delusion, the false absolutization of self and others. This places us in a futile rage against the universe (as if the universe has nothing better to do than go after us).
>
> The egocentric, alienated person thinks this impossible situation can be solved by pumping up the self to destroy the universe. But that's like Brer Rabbit attacking the Tar-Baby, trying to break free but only getting more and more stuck. Anger's wild energy is not the problem. It is simply raw energy. When directed by wisdom

instead of delusion, it can be turned against the real bars of the prison, namely, the delusions that falsely separate us from the universe.[2]

The separate self is the self trapped in its own drama and belief system. Spinning dramas is what this self does. This is how narrow mind functions. But believing the drama to be other than a story is the trap that imprisons you in narrow mind. Anger is how we spring that trap.

Before we proceed to ways to cool the fires of anger, let's make sure we have defined anger properly. There is such a thing as constructive or righteous anger. This is anger at injustice that leads to crusades for justice. Would we want to get rid of this kind of anger?

I am tempted to say, "No, such anger is good." But that is too simple a response. If your anger is fed by a belief in your victimization, it cannot help but split your world into good and evil, us and them. You may be the victim, but you are the good guy, and getting back at the bad guy is only just and right. This belief fuels all kinds of evil in the world.

Anger can direct your attention to injustice, and that is good. Once you see the injustice, however, why do you need to sustain the anger? Let it go and engage the injustice with a more clear and wise mind. But how do we let it go? Thurman draws his guidance from the eighth-century Buddhist teacher Shantideva, who used anger against itself in order to shatter its hold on us.

Shantideva's anger yoga, like all yogas, is rooted in spacious mind. You watch the anger without feeding it or starving it. In watching anger, you will see how it depends on a drama. Once the drama is recognized for what it is—just another belief narrow mind conjures up to maintain its sense of self and self-importance—the energy is channeled into ending the story and thus ending your suffering at the hands of the story, rather than inadvertently feeding the story by focusing your energy on the imaginary enemy. You see that the canoe is empty and that you are not the target. And with that realization, the anger fades and compassion and kindness blossom.

Alan Wallace, another contemporary Buddhist teacher, shares this story:

> Imagine walking along a sidewalk with your arms full of groceries, and someone roughly bumps into you so that you fall and your groceries are strewn over the ground. As you rise up from the puddle of broken eggs and tomato juice, you are ready to shout out, "You idiot! What's wrong with you? Are you blind?" But just before you can catch your breath to speak, you see that the person who bumped into you actually is blind. He, too, is sprawled in the spilled groceries, and your anger vanishes in an instant, to be replaced by sympathetic concern: "Are you hurt? Can I help you?" Our situation is like that. When we clearly realize that the source of disharmony and misery in the world is ignorance, we can open the door of wisdom and compassion.[3]

OPENING WISDOM'S DOOR

Anger keeps us from opening the door to wisdom. It does so by keeping us locked in the tiny closet of narrow mind that justifies anger by insisting that we are the target. One of the best ways I know of maintaining spaciousness and avoiding anger is taught by the thirteenth-century Spanish mystic Rabbi Moshe ben Nachman (also called Ramban and Nachmanides) in a short essay called *Iggeret haMussar,* the Letter of Ethical Discipline, written to his son in 1267.

Ramban wrote the *Iggeret haMussar* at the age of seventy-two while living in Acco, not far from modern-day Haifa, Israel. The letter was printed for the first time in Mantua, Italy, in 1623 as part of a prayer book compiled by Rabbi Yechiel Mili. Since that time, it has been reprinted and included in weekly and High Holy Day prayer books, and in collections of Psalms, as well as by itself. Ramban urged his son to read this letter weekly and to practice its teachings daily. I would encourage you to follow his advice as well.

To help with this task, I have recast the letter, updating the translation and integrating commentary within the body of the letter to make it easier to understand. I have tried to present the commentary in the same style as the letter to help maintain the flow of Ramban's original. The italicized material is my translation of Ramban's letter; the rest is my commentary on it.

AVOIDING ANGER THROUGH ETHICAL DISCIPLINE

Listen carefully to the discipline of your father and do not abandon the guidance of your mother [Proverbs 1:8]. The voice of the father speaks of law and principle. Without these, there is no direction. The voice of the mother speaks of situations, relationships, and applications. Without these, there is no meaning. You need both direction and meaning to shape a life rooted in lovingkindness.

Make it a habit to speak gently to all people at all times. Habits are created from willful action. You must choose your actions moment to moment. Yet in time, when one or another action becomes second nature to you, it happens almost of itself. This is the habit of which I speak. Don't imagine that lovingkindness just happens; it is built on actions we choose to perform. Choose to speak gently to all people at all times, and in time gentleness will become a habit.

This will protect you from anger. Anger is a danger to you, for it leads to grievous error. Anger clouds your judgment, and mistakes your personal desires for divine imperatives. Anger blinds you to unity and traps you in the illusion of separation and selfishness. Anger allows the echoed *I am* of ego to drown out the original *I AM* of God, causing you to fall into the most subtle idolatry, the worship of the sovereign self.

Our Rabbis taught, Whoever flares up in anger is subject to the discipline of Gehinnom [*Nedarim* 22a]. Hell (*Gehinnom*) is the sense of separation that arises with anger. Anger denies the fundamental unity of all things in, with, and as God. Anger pulls you "apart from" when in fact you are always "a part of." Anger allows you to destroy another by convincing you there is an "other" to destroy.

When you are trapped in the hell of alienation and separatism, you fall into despair. Despair (des-pair) means to uncouple, to break the unity of part and whole, not literally—for in fact the unity of all in All cannot be broken—but psychologically so that you feel cut off from life. Despairing of life, you despair of God, and find no purpose in living. At first anger feeds the self, setting the ego up as an idol to be worshiped. But worshiping the self is empty, and thus anger is replaced by despair, leaving you with a hollow god incapable of hallowing life. You are plunged into a downward spiral of ever-thickening darkness and hopelessness.

Thus it is written, Banish anger from your heart and remove evil from your flesh [Ecclesiastes 11:10]. *The evil mentioned here refers to Gehinnom, as it is written,"And the wicked are destined for the day of evil"* [Proverbs 16:4]. To banish anger is not easy. Anger, like all feelings, arises without warning and seems to possess you like a dybbuk (demon). This dybbuk comes from identifying with your feelings, mistaking the one who feels for the feelings themselves. Feelings arise naturally within you, but you must not mistake what you feel for who you are. Rather, be like the lake that reflects all things and yet is not identified with them. Or like the vast sky that holds clouds both stormy and calm, yet is not limited to them.

Feelings come and go; they fade with time. It is impossible to cling to them successfully. Joy and sadness, anger and love—

they are passing clouds on the clear sky of mind. Allow your feelings to be what they are, but do not mistake them for who you are. Thus, if you feel anger, see what you can learn from it, but do not identify with it.

Once you have distanced yourself from anger, the quality of humility will enter your heart. This sterling quality is the finest of all admirable traits, as it is written, "On the heels of humility comes the wonder of God" [Proverbs 22:4]. Humility is not a feeling per se; it is less a state of mind than a trait of character. Humility is an abiding awareness that arises within you when you discover the interconnectedness of all things.

Through humility, the wonder of God will intensify in your heart, for you will always be aware of where you have come from and where you are destined to go. You will realize that, in life, you are as transient as the maggot or the worm—all the more so in death.

Humility is the key to wonder. As humility grows, wonder deepens. You will see yourself as a temporary expression of God's infinite and timeless unfolding. Aware of your impermanence, you become brother and sister to all life. You realize the common fate of all beings and find in that realization a compassion that embraces all beings.

It is this sense of humility that reminds you of the One in Whom all your life unfolds—the Fountain of Glory of Whom it is written, "Behold heaven and the heaven of heavens cannot contain You, certainly not the hearts of humankind" [II Chronicles 6:18]. This Fountain of Glory is God, the infinite and formless Being who gives birth to the finite forms of becoming. God is the ocean and creation the waves. God is the sun and creation the rays of sunlight. God is the Source and the Substance. God is not a being among other beings, but Being Itself, the I AM that allows us to say "We are."

Everything is from God and of God, for there is only God. Thus it is written, "Do I [God] not fill heaven and earth?" [Jeremiah 23:24]. God is heaven and God is earth; there is nothing else.

After you give serious thought to these ideas, you will stand in awe of your Creator and will be guarded against error. Once you have acquired these fine qualities, you will indeed be happy with your lot. Standing in awe, experiencing the radical amazement that overwhelms you as you awaken to your unity with Reality, you are incapable of sin. Sin is the willful imposition of your will on the Divine Will. Ultimately you will fail, but much havoc is wreaked in the meantime. You can pit your will against the Divine Will only when you wrongly imagine you are not the Divine. When you play at being God rather than awaken to the truth that God is playing at being you, you try to control the world to suit your whim. This is the source of all human evil.

When you awaken to the unity of all in All, you discover that your will is now one with the Divine Will. What you now desire is the healing of the world through lovingkindness. You know what is right without choosing between right and wrong. You do good without having to reject evil. This is the new covenant spoken of by the prophet Jeremiah (31:30–34).

You are like a person suddenly tossed into the sea. The current pulls at you, the waves pound you. If you fight them, you drown. If you surrender to them, you float and can slowly make your way to shore. So too with humility and wonder.

When you stand in awe and wonder, you are suddenly cast into the sea that is God. There is a current. It is compassion and lovingkindness. There are waves. They are justice and righteousness. If you fight these, you will drown in despair. If you surrender to them, you will find yourself filled with the power of the sea to accomplish its goals.

You are created to accomplish the aims of God. To the extent that you mistake your personal desires for the aims of God, you are in error and open to sin. To the extent that you can empty yourself of your self and meet the One Who is the true you, you are in harmony with God and empowered by God.

When your actions display genuine humility—when you stand in solidarity with your fellows and in wonder of God; when you stand empty of self and the errors to which the self is prone—then the Divine is revealed within and around you; then you are alive to the glory of creation; then you live the life of the world to come.

Do not imagine that the world to come is tied to a future time. The world to come is present here and now, if only you open yourself to it. Speak gently and cultivate humility, and the wonder will embrace you; you will see and live the world to come here and now. Thus Rabbi Hanokh says, "Other nations too believe that there are two worlds. They too say: In the world to come. The difference is this: They think that the two worlds are separate and severed, but Israel professes that the two worlds are essentially one and shall in fact become one." The unity of this world and the world to come depends on you realizing your unity with all things in, with, and as God. This is what the Kotzker Rebbe tried to teach when he asked, "Where does God dwell?" Answering his own question, he said, "God dwells wherever you let God in." God is everywhere and everything, but until you are open to God in this way, God's infinity is blocked by the finitude of self.

As Martin Buber wrote, "It is said of a certain Talmudic master that the paths of heaven were as bright to him as the streets of his native town. Hasidism inverts the order: It is a greater thing if the streets of [your] native town are as bright to [you] as the paths of heaven. For it is here, where we stand, that we should try to make shine the light of the hidden divine life."[4]

Understand clearly that one who pretends to superiority over others rebels against God. Pride deludes you into separateness. You imagine that you are alone in the world. You imagine that you do for yourself in the world. You imagine that your success is yours alone. These are all lies and delusion. There is no "alone." You are a part of the other, and all are a part of the One.

If you have wealth, it is God who makes you prosperous. And if honor, does not honor belong to God? Wealth and honor come from God [I Chronicles 29:12]—*how can you glorify yourself with the honor of your Maker? If you take pride in wisdom, know that time may rob the most eloquent and wise speakers of their wisdom* [Job 12:20].

You do not become wealthy alone. At every step, others help you. Willingly or unwillingly, knowingly or unknowingly, you are aided at every turn. Your clothes—did you plant the cotton and harvest the crop? Did you spin the thread and weave the cloth? Did you bring it to market and stand long hours in hopes of a sale? No. Yet without the aid of those who did do all these things, you would have nothing to wear at all.

The same is true of the food you eat, the house in which you dwell, your job, even your wisdom. Nothing is yours alone. Nothing comes to you that does not come through the hands and minds of others. You owe these others a debt you can never repay.

From this debt humility grows. *Thus all people stand as equals before God. In time, the lofty may fall and the downtrodden rise up.* Owing the world leads to respecting the world. Knowing that you are who you are and have what you have by the grace and sweat and toil of others, you cannot help but embrace the world and all who dwell here with generosity, justice, and compassion.

Let your words be spoken gently, inviting the other to dialogue with you heart to heart. *Let your head be bowed* in greeting to all you pass. *Cast your eyes downward* so that you see what is around you, not imagining that anything is beneath your attention. *Cast your heart heavenward,* opening to the wonder of God who is the Source and Substance of all. *And when speaking, do not stare at your listener* as a ploy to intimidate him.

Recognize the greatness in even the lowliest of things. If another is wiser or wealthier than you, honor that wisdom and that wealth, but covet neither. And if another is poorer or less wise than you, consider that they may be more generous or righteous or compassionate than you, and again show respect. If another sins, remember that it may be through error or ignorance. If you sin, be not so quick to excuse your actions, but see if you are not willful and deliberate in violating the ways of righteousness.

In all your words, actions, and thoughts—at all times—imagine in your heart that you are standing in the presence of the Holy One, Source and Substance of all reality, and that the Divine Presence rests upon you. Indeed, the glory of God fills the universe.

This is not an abstraction, but a practice. Before you speak, imagine that you are speaking to God. Before you act, imagine that you are serving God. Before you utter a single word or perform a single deed, imagine that you stand before the One Who is all, for indeed it is so.

God is all; there is nothing else. When you speak, you are speaking to God. When you act, you are acting as God's agent. To know this is to awaken to the highest level of spirituality. To know this requires discipline. Discipline of speech, speaking gently. Discipline of deed, acting graciously and with respect. Discipline of thought, visualizing God in and as all things.

Speak reverently and with awe, ready to serve the way of righteousness. *Act with restraint in the company of others. If one should taunt you, do not answer defensively, but respond gently* in tones that invite dialogue and shared understanding. *Take care to study Torah diligently so that you will be able to fulfill its commands.* Torah is more than history, law, and legend. Torah is the wisdom of perfecting the self and the world with justice, kindness, and humility. Torah is not fixed, but alive and changing. It speaks directly to your heart, revealing just what it is you need to know to move one step closer to the holy person you can be.

Thus, when you arise from study, ponder carefully what you have learned; see what there is in it that you can put into practice. For there is little point to learning without living. Learn in order to act righteously, to transform the world and yourself with lovingkindness.

Cast external matters from your mind when you stand to pray; empty yourself of self that you might be filled with God. Carefully prepare your heart in the presence of the Holy One by visualizing the Divine around and within you. Empty your thoughts, focus your breathing, allow the gentle rhythm of the breath to quiet your mind, still your body, and release your soul from the delusion of separateness. And before you utter even a single word, consider deeply what you say, that your prayer might give voice to the universal yearning for gentleness, humility, and peace.

Conduct yourself in these ways in all your endeavors for as long as you live. In this way, you will surely avoid errors of will, word, and deed; your words, actions, and thoughts will be flawless. Your prayer will be pure and clear, sincere and open to God, the Source and Substance of all Being and Becoming, as it is written, "When You prepare their hearts to concentrate, You are attentive to their prayers" [Psalm 10:17].

Read this letter once a week and neglect none of it. Fulfill it and in so doing, walk forever in the ways of God. In this way you will succeed in your endeavors, for all you desire will be for the good. *In this way you will merit the world to come that lies hidden for the righteous,* for you will open your eyes and you will see that for those who hallow this world, this world reveals itself as the world to come.

Amen, Selah!

AN INVITATION TO BECOME A HIDDEN SAINT

In a place where there is no mensch, be a mensch.

—Hillel

A mensch is a person who puts others first. Putting others first might be called in Sanskrit *maitri bhavana,* the discipline *(bhavana)* of friendliness *(maitri).* It requires nothing more than paying attention to the needs of others, and doing what you can to help meet those needs. This encompasses animals as well as people.

> On a hot summer day, a man found a thirsty dog at the edge of a well, unable to reach the water. He said to himself, "This dog must be suffering from thirst as I am now." The man went into the well, filled his shoe with water and offered it to the dog to drink. God was pleased with him and granted him forgiveness of all his sins. The Prophet, peace be upon him, was asked: Messenger of God, are we rewarded for kindness to animals?" He said, "There is a reward for kindness to every living thing."[1]

One interfaith minister I met on a meditation retreat told me that her practice was friendliness. "My service to God is through befriending God's creation: human, animal, plant, and mineral. I once learned from a Jain teacher to walk with my eyes cast downward to make certain I did not step on any living creature. I have expanded that. I now look all around to see where I can avoid doing harm and perhaps do some good."

She then shared with me this Celtic prayer with which she starts each day:

ORTHA NAN GAIDHEAL PRAYER

> This morning, as I kindle the fire on my hearth,
> I pray that the flame of God's love may burn in my heart
>   and in the hearts of all I meet today.
> I pray that no envy or malice, no hatred or fear may smother
>   the flame.
> I pray that indifference and apathy, contempt and pride,
>   may not pour like cold water on the fire.
> Instead, may the spark of God's love light the love in my
>   heart, that it may burn brightly through the day.
> And may I warm those who are lonely, whose hearts are
>   cold and lifeless, so that all may know the comfort of
>   God's love.[2]

A rabbi I know devotes one day a week to simply being of service. She gets up in the morning and dedicates the day to God. She then leaves her home for the city close by and wanders about looking for ways to be of service to others. "I have no plan for the day, other than to be present to what needs doing and to do those things I can without pride or prejudice. Sometimes I will find myself helping someone move into or out of an apartment, or sitting with the homeless, or walking tourists to their destination. The idea is to be free of any idea other than to serve, to befriend, to be kind."

Each of these people is acting as a mensch. According to Talmudic legend, there are always thirty-six *menschen* (the plural of mensch) on the planet at any given moment (*Sanhedrin* 97b; *Sukkah* 45b). Without their acts of lovingkindness, life on this planet would implode under the weight of human selfishness, anger, ignorance, and greed.

The number thirty-six is, according to Jewish numerology, twice *chai,* eighteen, the Hebrew word for "life." These *menschen* are called *lamed-vavniks,* from the Hebrew letters *lamed* and *vav* that make up the number thirty-six. They live both for themselves and for others (twice *chai*), and the lovingkindness they generate keeps human beings from total annihilation. Cultivating the sacred art of lovingkindness is enrolling yourself in the ranks of the *lamed-vavniks.*

Although some may take the legend literally and place their faith and fate in these hidden saints and *bodhisattvas,* I, for one, cannot do so. I prefer to think of the teaching this way: The tipping point for maintaining human life on this planet is thirty-six people practicing the sacred art of lovingkindness at any given moment. These need not be the same thirty-six people at each moment, however. I believe that people step into and out of the *lamed-vavnik* role, and that at any given moment thirty-six people are stepping in.

Right now, at this very moment, there must be thirty-six acts of lovingkindness occurring on the planet, or the collective weight of human ignorance, fear, anger, and greed would crush humankind. The fact that you are reading this book and the world is still functioning means that someone, or rather thirty-six someones, are carrying out the *lamed-vavnik* obligation.

But what about the next moment? Can you really afford to let your very existence and the existence of the entire world rest on the shoulders of others? Or should you consciously pitch in and take up the challenge of being a *lamed-vavnik* yourself? And, if you do choose to step in, can you afford to do so alone, or should you bring a few others along with you?

BECOMING A *LAMED-VAVNIK*

I want to conclude this book with an offer. I want you to enlist in the *Lamed-Vav* Society, an international network of hidden saints who devote themselves to the sacred art of lovingkindness. Since they are hidden, of course, I have no way of proving that such a society exists, so your local chapter may be the only chapter, but I doubt it.

There are no dues for membership, but there are a few rules. The first is to set your intention to practice the sacred art of lovingkindness daily, and to cultivate the Thirteen Attributes: (1) realizing the divinity of self, (2) realizing the divinity of other, (3) cultivating creativity, (4) engendering compassion, (5) finding grace, (6) acting with equanimity, (7) creating kindness, (8) bringing forth truth, (9) preserving kindness, (10) forgiving iniquity, (11) forgiving willfulness, (12) forgiving error, and (13) cleansing yourself of delusion.

The second rule of the *Lamed-Vav* Society is that in addition to daily practice, you choose one day a week to fully take on the mantle of the *lamed-vavnik*. You spend this day looking to be of service to others in a manner than cultivates lovingkindness in your community. This may mean you choose to volunteer as a Big Sister or Big Brother once a week, or it may mean you volunteer at a homeless shelter or hospital, or it may mean that you simply decide that each Tuesday, to pick one day at random, you will consciously look for opportunities to put others first regardless of how it impacts your goals for the day.

The third rule is to recruit others. Share the legend of the *lamed-vavniks* with people and invite them to "sign up." If you have children, they are the first people to recruit. You can make your family a chapter of the *Lamed-Vav* Society. Each member of the family can choose her or his day for *Lamed-Vav* service and share how the day went with other family members over dinner or at bedtime. In addition you can take one attribute of the thirteen and make that a subject for the week's table talk and daily practice.

If you are a teacher, you can create a *Lamed-Vav* classroom where each student picks a lovingkindness day, and students share their experiences with one another once a week. Friends can do the same. The point is that it is more fun to find a few not-so-hidden saints to hang out with and to lean on.

I could go on listing examples, but I suspect you can do this on your own. Once you realize that the whole world depends on you for its very survival, you will not lack in opportunities to serve. Just remember that you are a hidden saint. While it is fine to invite others to join with you, make sure you don't advertise your own saintliness. While being a *lamed-vavnik* may be good for your soul, it doesn't belong on a resume.

NOTES

CHAPTER TWO

1. Matthew Fox, *Creativity* (New York: Jeremy P. Tarcher, 2004), p. 47.
2. Ibid., p. 116.
3. Martin Buber, *The Way of Man according to the Teaching of Hasidism* (Secaucus, N.J.: Carol Publishing Group, 1994), p. 16.
4. Ibid.
5. *Gospel of Thomas* 70.
6. Ibid., 113.
7. Ibid., 77.
8. J. Krishnamurti, *The Awakening of Intelligence* (New York: Harper and Row, 1987), p. 479.

CHAPTER THREE

1. Marc Ian Barasch, *Field Notes on the Compassionate Life* (New York: Rodale, 2005), p. 3.
2. Ibid.
3. Sharon Salzberg, *Lovingkindness* (Boston: Shambhala, 2002), p. 24.
4. Ibid., pp. 21–22.
5. Eknath Easwaran, *God Makes the Rivers to Flow* (Tomales, Calif.: Nilgiri Press, 1991), p. 104.

CHAPTER FOUR

1. Walpola Rahula, *What the Buddha Taught* (London: Gordon Fraser Gallery, 1978), p. 111.
2. Wayne Muller, *Sabbath: Remembering the Sacred Rhythm of Rest and Delight* (New York: Bantam Books, 2000), p. 12.

CHAPTER FIVE

1. Chogyam Trungpa, *Training the Mind and Cultivating Lovingkindness* (Boston: Shambhala, 2005), p. 61–62.

CHAPTER SIX

1. Albert Camus, cited in Jack Kornfield, *The Art of Forgiveness, Lovingkindness, and Peace* (New York: Bantam Books, 2004), p. 78.
2. Gregg Krech, ToDo website, www.todoinstitute.org.

CHAPTER SEVEN

1. Jack Kornfield, *The Art of Forgiveness, Lovingkindness, and Peace* (New York: Bantam, 2004), p. 34.
2. J. Krishnamurti, *Freedom from the Known* (New York: HarperCollins, 1969), p. 119.

CHAPTER EIGHT

1. Jack Riemer and Nathaniel Stampfer, *So That Your Values Live On: Ethical Wills and How to Prepare Them* (Woodstock, Vt.: Jewish Lights Publishing, 1991), p. xvii.

CHAPTER ELEVEN

1. Laura Huxley, *You Are Not the Target* (New York: Marlowe & Company, 1998).
2. Robert Thurman, *Breathe Magazine* (September/October) 2005.
3. Cited in Kornfield, *Art of Forgiveness*, p. 36.
4. Buber, *The Way of Man*, p. 38.

CONCLUSION

1. Camille Helminski, ed., *The Book of Character* (Santa Cruz, Calif.: The Book Foundation, 2004), p. 72.
2. The *Ortha Nan Gaidheal*, Celtic Christian prayer, translated by Alexander Carmichael, in Eknath Easwaran, *God Makes the Rivers to Flow* (Tomales, Calif.: Nilgiri Press, 2003), p. 151.

SUGGESTIONS FOR FURTHER READING

Barasch, Marc Ian. *Field Notes on the Compassionate Life*. New York: Rodale, 2005.

Boorstein, Sylvia. *Pay Attention, for Goodness' Sake*. New York: Ballantine, 2002.

Borg, Marcus J. *Meeting Jesus Again for the First Time*. San Francisco: HarperSanFrancisco, 1994.

Buber, Martin. *The Way of Man according to the Teaching of Hasidism*. New York: Citadel Press, 1996.

Chaim, Chofetz. *Ahavath Chesed*. New York: Feldheim, 1976.

Childre, Doc. *Transforming Anger*. Oakland, Ca.: New Harbinger, 2003.

Chödrön, Pema. *Awakening Lovingkindness*. Boston: Shambhala Press, 1996.

———. *Start Where You Are*. Boston: Shambhala Press, 2001.

———. *The Wisdom of No Escape*. Boston: Shambhala Press, 2001.

Cordovero, Moshe. *Palm Tree of Devorah*. Jerusalem: Targum, 1993.

Dalai Lama. *The Compassionate Life*. Boston: Wisdom, 2003.

———. *The Good Heart*. Boston: Wisdom, 1996.

———. *Healing Anger*. Ithaca, N.Y.: Snow Lion, 1997.

Dresner, Samuel H. *Levi Yitzhak of Berditchev: Portrait of a Hasidic Master*. New York: Shapolsky, 1986.

Easwaran, Eknath. *Meditation*. Tomales, Ca.: Nilgiri Press, 1991.

———. *God Makes the Rivers to Flow*. Tomales, Ca.: Nilgiri Press, 2003.

Eppsteiner, Fred, ed. *The Path of Compassion: Writings on Socially Engaged Buddhism*. Berkeley: Parallax Press, 1988.

Feldman, Christina. *Compassion: Listening to the Cries of the World*. Berkeley: Rodmell Press, 2005.

Ford, Marcia. *Finding Hope: Cultivating God's Gift of a Hopeful Spirit*. Woodstock, Vt.: SkyLight Paths, 2006.

————. *The Sacred Art of Forgiveness: Forgiving Ourselves and Others through God's Grace*. Woodstock, Vt.: SkyLight Paths, 2006.

Fox, Matthew. *Creativity*. New York: Jeremy P. Tarcher, 2004.

Goleman, Daniel. *Destructive Emotions: How Can We Overcome Them?* New York: Bantam Books, 2003.

Helminski, Camille. *Book of Character*. Watsonville, Ca.: Book Foundation, 2004.

————. *Book of Revelations*. Watsonville, Ca.: Book Foundation, 2004.

Helminski, Kabir. *Living Presence*. New York: Jeremy P. Tarcher, 1992.

Huxley, Laura. *You Are Not the Target*. New York: Marlowe, 1998.

Karcher, Stephen. *How to Use the I Ching*. New York: Element Books, 1997.

Katie, Byron. *Loving What Is*. New York: Three Rivers Press, 2003.

Kedar, Karyn D. *The Bridge to Forgiveness: Stories and Prayers for Finding God and Restoring Wholeness*. Woodstock, Vt.: Jewish Lights, 2007.

Kierkgaard, Søren. *Works of Love*. Edited and translated by Howard V. Hong and Edna H. Hong. Princeton, N.J.: Princeton University Press, 1995.

Kornfield, Jack. *The Art of Forgiveness, Lovingkindness, and Peace*. New York: Bantam Books, 2004.

Krech, Gregg. *Naikan: Gratitude, Grace, and the Japanese Art of Self-Reflection*. Berkeley: Stone Bridge Press, 2001.

Krishnamurti, Jiddu. *Freedom from the Known*. San Francisco: HarperSanFrancisco, 1975.

————. *The Awakening of Intelligence*. San Francisco: HarperSanFrancisco, 1987.

Lindahl, Kay. *Practicing the Sacred Art of Listening: A Guide to Enrich Your Relationships and Kindle Your Spiritual Life*. Woodstock, Vt: SkyLight Paths, 2003.

————. *The Sacred Art of Listening: Forty Reflections for Cultivating a Spiritual Practice*. Woodstock, Vt: SkyLight Paths, 2002.

Marshall, Jay. *Thanking & Blessing—The Sacred Art: Spiritual Vitality through Gratefulness*. Woodstock, Vt.: SkyLight Paths, 2007.

May, Rollo. *The Courage to Create*. New York: W.W. Norton, 1975.

Muller, Wayne. *Sabbath*. New York: Bantam Books, 2000.

Prager, Dennis. *Happiness Is a Serious Problem*. New York: Regan Books, 1999.

Rahula, Walpola. *What the Buddha Taught*. London: Gordon Fraser Gallery, 1978.

Ramban. *A Letter for the Ages*. Translated by Rabbi Avrohom Chaim Feuer. Brooklyn: Mesorah, 2001.

Reynolds, David. *A Handbook for Constructive Living*. Honolulu: University of Hawaii Press, 2002.

Riemer, Jack, and Nathaniel Stampfer. *So That Your Values Live On: Ethical Wills and How to Prepare Them*. Woodstock, Vt.: Jewish Lights, 1993.

Salzberg, Sharon. *Lovingkindness*. Boston: Shambhala Press, 1995.

———. *The Force of Kindness*. Boulder: SoundsTrue, 2005.

Sawyer, Nanette. *Hospitality—The Sacred Art: Discovering the Hidden Spiritual Power of Invitation and Welcome*. Woodstock, Vt.: SkyLight Paths, 2007.

Schneersohn, Shalom DovBer. *On Ahavas Yisrael* (Love of Israel). New York: Kehot, 1996.

Shantideva. *The Way of the Bodhisattva*. Translated by Padmakara Translation Group. Boston: Shambhala Press, 2003.

Shapiro, Rami. *Letter of Ethical Discipline: A New Reading of Iggeret HaKodesh*. Miami: Light House Books, 1994.

———. *Ethics of the Sages:* Pirke Avot—*Annotated and Explained*. Woodstock, Vt.: SkyLight Paths, 2006.

———. *Hasidic Tales: Annotated and Explained*. Woodstock, Vt.: SkyLight Paths, 2004.

———. *The Hebrew Prophets: Selections Annotated and Explained*. Woodstock, Vt.: SkyLight Paths, 2004.

Templeton, Sir John. *Agape Love*. Philadelphia: Templeton Foundation, 1999.

Trungpa, Chogyam. *Training the Mind and Cultivating Loving-kindness*. Boston: Shambhala Press, 2005.

Twerski, Abraham J. *Happiness and the Human Spirit: The Spirituality of Becoming the Best You Can Be*. Woodstock, Vt.: Jewish Lights, 2007.

INDEX OF PRAYERS AND PRACTICES

ACKNOWLEDGMENTS

Emily Wichland, my editor at SkyLight Paths, suggested this book to me. I thought it would be an interesting exercise and not too challenging. I was wrong. Like most books I write, I start out thinking I know what I am going to say, only to discover that I actually have little or nothing pertinent to say at all. The more I delved into the topic of lovingkindness, the more coarse my life seemed to be; the writing slowed to a crawl and I seriously thought about abandoning the book. Emily was encouraging and generous, giving me more time to work through the issues that made writing the book so difficult. Then it was her turn to be overwhelmed; the book needed lots of editing. She enlisted the help of yet another SkyLight Paths editor, Maura Shaw, and the three of us struggled to free the insights buried in my original manuscript. So what you have here is a collaboration. Any flaws in the book are mine alone, but what value you may find in these pages is due to their diligence and grace. Thank you, Emily and Maura, for making this book as good as it is.